THE NEEDS OF STRANGERS

ALSO BY MICHAEL IGNATIEFF

Virtual War: Kosovo and Beyond

Isaiah Berlin: A Life

The Warrior's Honor: Ethnic War and Modern Conscience

Scar Tissue

Blood and Belonging: Journeys into the New Nationalism

The Russian Album

A Just Measure of Pain

Michael Ignatieff

THE NEEDS
OF STRANGERS

Picador USA
Metropolitan Books
Henry Holt and Company
New York

www.picadorusa.com

Picador® is a U.S. registered trademark and is used by Henry Holt and Company under license from Pan Books Limited.

For information on Picador USA Reading Group Guides, as well as ordering, please contact the Trade Marketing department at St. Martin's Press.
Phone: 1-800-221-7945 extension 763
Fax: 212-677-7456
E-mail: trademarketing@stmartins.com

Grateful acknowledgment is made to J. M. Dent & Sons Ltd for permission to reprint extracts from the Everyman's Library edition of J. J. Rousseau's *The Social Contract and Discourses*, 1973, and to the Prado Museum for permission to reprint a detail from "The Haywain," by Hieronymus Bosch.

ISBN 0-312-28180-3

First published in the United States by Viking Penguin Inc.

First Picador USA Edition: June 2001

10 9 8 7 6 5 4 3 2 1

CONTENTS

gave up Christian religion → went back
"Confessions"
Manichaeism
rhetoric

French mathematician
philosopher
Jansenism
reason can't solve
difficulties or satisfy
hope

Flemish painter
Folk legend's
grotesque

Dutch humanist
sharp humor
attacked clerical abuse

remained Roman Catholic
attacked Luther

background

scottish philosopher
no reason, belief

historian

scottish author
genius at biography

humanity good by nature, corrupted
by society

scottish economist
division of labor, oppose monopolies

Marx, Freud

market
metaphysics
need

Full name, dates of birth + death, major work(s), reason
it's important

ACKNOWLEDGEMENTS

During the years I was thinking about this book, I was a senior research fellow at King's College, Cambridge. I want to thank the Managers of the Research Centre, the Provost, Bernard Williams, and the fellows of the college for the honour and pleasure of their company.
I would like to thank those who commented on the manuscript and who helped me to see my way with this project: Hugh Brody, Sylvana Tomaselli, John Forrester, Istvan Hont, Gareth Stedman Jones, Judith Shklar, William Leiss, Jan Dalley, Mike Petty, Elisabeth Sifton, Anthony Sheil, Geoffrey Hawthorn.

The book is dedicated to Susan – who teaches me my needs.

INTRODUCTION:
TRAGEDY AND UTOPIA

*There are few things we should keenly desire
if we really knew what we wanted.*

LA ROCHEFOUCAULD

I live in a market street in north London. Every Tuesday morning there is a barrow outside my door and a cluster of old age pensioners rummage through the torn curtains, buttonless shirts, stained vests, torn jackets, frayed trousers and faded dresses that the barrow man has on offer. They make a cheerful chatter outside my door, beating down the barrow man's prices, scrabbling for bargains like crows pecking among the stubble.

They are not destitute, just respectably poor. The old men seem more neglected than the women: their faces are grey and unshaven and their necks hang loose inside yellowed shirt collars. Their old bodies must be thin and white beneath their clothes. The women seem more self-possessed, as if old age were something their mothers had prepared them for. They also have the skills for poverty: the hems of their coats are neatly darned, their buttons are still in place.

These people give the impression of having buried their wives and husbands long ago and having watched their children decamp to the suburbs. I imagine them living alone in small dark rooms lit by the glow of electric heaters. I came upon one old man once doing his shopping alone, weighed down in a queue at a potato stall and nearly fainting from tiredness. I made him sit down in a pub while I did the rest of his shopping. But if he needed my help, he certainly didn't want it. He was clinging on to his life, gasping for breath, but he stared straight ahead when we talked and his fingers would not be pried from his burdens. All these old people seem like that, cut adrift from family, slipping away into the dwindling realm of their inner voices, clinging to the old barrow as if it were a raft carrying them out to sea.

My encounters with them are a parable of moral relations between strangers in the welfare state. They have needs, and because they live within a welfare state, these needs confer entitlements—rights—to the resources of people like me.[1] Their needs and their entitlements establish a silent relation between us. As we stand together in line at the post office, while they cash their pension cheques, some tiny portion of my income is transferred into their pockets through the numberless capillaries of the state. The mediated quality of our relationship seems necessary to both of us. They are dependent on the state, not upon me, and we are both glad of it. Yet I am also aware of how this mediation walls us off from each other. We are responsible for each other, but we are not responsible to each other.

My responsibilities towards them are mediated through a vast division of labour. In my name a social worker climbs the stairs to their rooms and makes sure they are as warm and as clean as they can be persuaded to be. When they get too old to go out, a volunteer will bring them a hot meal, make up their beds, and if the volunteer is a compassionate person, listen to their whispering streams of memory. When they can't go on, an ambulance will take them to the hospital, and when they die, a nurse will be there to listen to the ebbing of their breath. It is this solidarity among strangers, this transformation through the division of labour of needs into rights and rights into care that gives us whatever fragile basis we have for saying that we live in a moral community.

Modern welfare may not be generous by any standard other than a comparison with the nineteenth-century workhouse, but it does attempt to satisfy a wide range of basic needs for food, shelter, clothing, warmth and medical care. The question is whether that is all a human being needs. When we talk about needs we mean something more than just the basic necessities of human survival. We also use the word to describe what a person needs in order to live to their full potential. What we need in order to survive, and what we need in order to flourish are two different things. The aged poor on my street get just enough to survive. The question is whether they get what they need in order to live a human life.

The political arguments between right and left over the future of the welfare state which rage over these old people's heads almost always take their needs entirely for granted. Both sides assume that what they need is income, food, clothing, shelter and medical care, then debate whether they are entitled to these goods as a matter of right, and whether there are adequate resources to provide them if they are. What almost never gets asked is whether they might need something more than the means of mere survival.

There are good reasons for this silence. It is difficult enough to define human need in terms of basic necessities. These are, after all, relative and historical, and there has always been fierce controversy over the level at which basic human entitlements should be set in any society. How much more controversial must be the definition of need as the conditions for human flourishing. There is not just one good human life, but many. Who is to say what humans need to accomplish all the finest purposes they can set for themselves?

It is also notorious how self-deceiving we are about our needs. By definition, a person must know that he desires something. It is quite possible, on the other hand, to be in need of something and not know that one is. Just as we often desire what we do not need, so we often need what we do not consciously desire.

If we often deceive ourselves about what we need, we are likely to be deceived about what strangers need. There are few presumptions in human relations more dangerous than the idea that one knows what another human being needs better than they do themselves. In politics, this presumption is a warrant to ignore democratic preferences and to trample on freedom. In other realms too, the arrogation of the right by doctors to define the needs of their patients, of social workers to administer the needs of their clients, and finally of parents to decide the needs of their children is in each case a warrant for abuse.

Yet if we are often deceived about our own needs, there must be cases in which it is in our interest that someone speaks for our needs when we ourselves cannot. There are people who have had to survive on so little for so long in our society that their needs have withered away to barest necessity. Is it wrong to raise their expectations, to give them a sense of the things they have gone without? Is it wrong to argue that the strangers at my door should not be content with the scraps at the barrow? Any politics which wants to improve the conditions of their lives has to speak for needs which they themselves may not be able to articulate. That is why politics is such a dangerous business: to mobilize a majority for change you must raise expectations and create needs which leap beyond the confines of existing reality. To create needs is to create discontent, and to invite disillusionment. It is to play with lives and hopes. The only safeguard in this dangerous game is the democratic requirement of informed consent. One has no right to speak for needs which those one represents cannot intelligibly recognize as their own.

This was the first question I began with: when is it right to speak for the needs of strangers? Politics is not only the art of representing the needs of strangers; it is also the perilous business of speaking on behalf of needs which strangers have had no chance to articulate on their own.

The second question I asked myself was whether it was possible to define what human beings need in order to flourish. The representation of the needs of strangers would not merely be perilous, it would be impossible, if human needs were infinitely contestable. In fact politics as such would be impossible unless individual preferences could recognize themselves and unite under a common banner of need. Consistent moral behaviour itself would be impossible unless there were some minimum degree of agreement, within a given society, as to the necessary preconditions of human flourishing.

The distinction I want to make is also one between needs

which can be specified in a language of political and social rights and those which cannot. Most arguments in politics these days are about the first sort of needs, for food, shelter, clothing, education and employment. The conservative counter-attack on the welfare state is above all an attack on the idea that these needs make rights; an attack on this idea puts into question the very notion of a society as a moral community.

In the attempt to defend the principle that needs do make rights, it is possible to forget about the range of needs which cannot be specified as rights and to let them slip out of the language of politics. Rights language offers a rich vernacular for the claims an individual may make on or against the collectivity, but it is relatively impoverished as a means of expressing individuals' needs *for* the collectivity. It can only express the human ideal of fraternity as mutual respect for rights, and it can only defend the claim to be treated with dignity in terms of our common identity as rights-bearing creatures. Yet we are more than rights-bearing creatures, and there is more to respect in a person than his rights. The administrative good conscience of our time seems to consist in respecting individuals' rights while demeaning them as persons. In the best of our prisons and psychiatric hospitals, for example, inmates are fed, clothed and housed in adequate fashion; the visits of lawyers and relatives are not stopped; the cuffs and clubs are kept in the guard house. Those needs which can be specified in rights are more or less respected. Yet every waking hour, inmates may still feel the silent contempt of authority in a glance, gesture or procedure. The strangers at my door have welfare rights, but it is another question altogether whether they have the respect and consideration of the officials who administer these rights.

It is because money cannot buy the human gestures which confer respect, nor rights guarantee them as entitlements, that any decent society requires a public discourse about the needs of the human person. It is because fraternity, love, belonging, dignity and respect cannot be specified as rights that we ought to specify them as needs and seek, with the blunt institutional procedures at our disposal, to make their satisfaction a routine human practice. At the very least, if we had a language of needs at our disposal, we would be in a better position to understand the difference between granting people their rights and giving people what they need.

I am saying that a decent and humane society requires a shared language of the good. The one our society lives by – a language of rights – has no terms for those dimensions of the human good which require acts of virtue unspecifiable as a legal or civil obligation.

A theory of human needs is a particular kind of language of the human good. To define human nature in terms of needs is to define what we *are* in terms of what we *lack*, to insist on the distinctive emptiness and incompleteness of humans as a species. As natural creatures, we are potential only. There is nothing intrinsic to our natures which entitles us to anything. Yet we are the only species with the capacity to create and transform our needs, the only species whose needs have a history. It is the needs we have created for ourselves, and the language of entitlements we have derived from them, which give us any claim to respect and dignity as a species, and as individuals. Needs language, therefore, is a distinctively historical and relative language of the human good.

It is also, in principle, a non-teleological language. If human nature is historical, there cannot be any ultimate state of human fulfilment that corresponds to the attainment of the human good as such. The only human goods which a needs language can specify are those absolute prerequisites for any human pursuit. If we need love, respect, fraternity, it is not because these are required for the realization of our essential natures, but because whatever we choose to do with our lives, we can scarcely be reconciled to ourselves and to others without them.

It is common in the language of rights to define essential requirements – 'basic goods', as John Rawls calls them – as necessary preconditions for personal freedom.[2] The advantage of this way of thinking is that it seeks to reconcile a theory of the good with the freedom of each individual to live his life as he chooses. The disadvantage is that many essential requirements of a decent life – love, respect, solidarity with others – cannot be sensibly justified as necessary for personal freedom. I don't need to be loved in order to be free; I need to be loved to be at peace with myself and to be able to love in turn. A theory of the human good cannot, I think, be premissed on the absolute priority of liberty.

Nor can it be based on the priority of happiness as the ultimate human end. If we need love, it is for reasons which go beyond the happiness it brings; it is for the connection, the rootedness, it gives us with others. Many of the things we need most deeply in life – love chief among them – do not necessarily bring us happiness. If we need them, it is to go to the depth of our being, to learn as much of ourselves as we can stand, to be reconciled to what we find in ourselves and in those around us.

In the end, a theory of human needs has to be premissed on some set of choices about what humans need in order to be human: not what they need to be happy or free, since these are subsidiary goals, but what they need in order to realize the full extent of their potential. There cannot be any eternally valid account of what it means to be human. All we have to go on is the historical record of what men have valued most in human life.

There does exist a set of words for these needs – love, respect, honour, dignity, solidarity with others. The problem is that their meanings have been worn out with casual over-use in politics. They have been cheapened, not only by easy rhetoric, but also by the easy assumption that if a society manages to meet the basic survival needs of its people, it also goes some way towards meeting these more intangible needs. Yet the relation between what we need in order to survive and what we need in order to flourish is more complicated than that. Giving the aged poor their pension and providing them with medical care may be a necessary condition for their self-respect and their dignity, but it is not a sufficient condition. It is the manner of the giving that counts and the moral basis on which it is given: whether strangers at my door get their stories listened to by the social worker, whether the ambulance man takes care not to jostle them when they are taken down the steep stairs of their apartment building, whether a nurse sits with them in the hospital when they are frightened and alone. Respect and dignity are conferred by gestures such as these. They are gestures too much a matter of human art to be made a consistent matter of administrative routine.

Respect and dignity also depend on whether entitlements are understood to be a matter of right, a matter of deserving, or a matter of charity. In many Western welfare states, entitlements are still perceived both by the giver and the receiver, as gifts. To be in need, to be in receipt of welfare, is still understood as a source of shame. Needs may make rights in law, but they do not necessarily make rights in the minds of the strangers at my door.

There is also a contradiction, at the heart of the welfare state, between the respect we owe persons as individuals and as fellow human beings. In the first case, respect is owed to their specific qualities as individuals; in the second, to their common humanity. The first type of respect requires us to treat them differently, unequally; the second, to treat them exactly like every other human being. In the welfare state, individuals are supposed to be treated equally, as if their needs were all the same. Yet our needs are not the same: what respect means to you may not be what respect means to me. Besides, all individuals are not due the same kind of respect as individuals. Treating everyone as if their needs were the same may be a necessary condition, but it is not a sufficient condition for treating *each* of them with respect. It is an open question whether any welfare system can reconcile this contradiction between treating individuals equally and treating individuals with respect. The most common criticism of modern welfare is precisely that in treating everyone the same it ends up treating everyone like a thing.

This kind of difficulty opened up the third question which came to concern me when writing this book. Might there not be some needs, like our need for respect, which cannot be satisfied by collective social provision except at some cost to other needs, like our need to be treated equally? A potential contradiction of the same sort arises between our need for social solidarity and our need for freedom. The individualist bias of our language of rights and entitlements makes it difficult to grasp this contradiction, but it is a fundamental one. We not only have needs for ourselves, we have needs on behalf of others. Many of those lucky or rich enough to be adequately clothed, fed and housed themselves feel the lack of these things among their fellow citizens as a blight upon their possessions.

This is something more than social conscience. Individuals are not solitary masters of pre-given preferences; what others need and what they lack are constitutive of their own needs. It is as common for us to need things on behalf of others, to need good schools for the sake of our children, safe streets for the sake of our neighbours, decent old people's homes for the strangers at our door, as it is for us to need them for ourselves. The deepest motivational springs of political involvement are to be located in this human capacity to feel needs for others.

The welfare state enacts this need for solidarity yet also ensures that those with resources and those in need remain strangers to each other. There are those, like Ivan Illich, who claim that a social division of labour and social solidarity are incompatible.[3] We will have to dismantle the edifice of state welfare if we wish to cease being moral strangers to each other. Yet I doubt that the pensioners at my door want to return to the days when they were dependent on the fickle mercy of their sons and daughters or the uncertain charity of philanthropy. The bureaucratized transfer of income among strangers has freed each of us from the enslavement of gift relations. Yet if the welfare state does serve the needs of freedom, it does not serve the needs of solidarity. We remain a society of strangers.

The obvious question, however, is whether societies can ever reconcile freedom and solidarity. The societies which have marched under Marx's banner – 'from each according to his abilities, to each according to his needs' – have all turned out to be disastrous for liberty.

Faced with this evidence, liberals by and large believe that one has to choose among the needs which one wishes to satisfy in politics. One can either have a society in which individuals are free to choose their needs as they see fit – such a society is unlikely to be rich in relations of solidarity – or one can choose a society which makes the determination and satisfaction of need a matter of collective social choice. In this case, there is a risk that individuals will cease to be free. Given these choices, liberals by and large choose liberty over solidarity. Socialists on the other hand insist that these needs are not in ultimate contradiction; they hold to a vision in which liberty and solidarity are reconciled, in which human beings can have needs for themselves and needs for the sake of others and satisfy both equally. To call such a vision utopian is not to demean it, but merely to observe that no socialist society has yet managed to reconcile these antinomies.

The utopian tradition in politics not only claims that needs are not in contradiction, it would also claim that there are no human needs which cannot be satisfied by collective social provision. One of the purposes of this book is to inquire whether this is true in principle. Love, for example, is perhaps the most desperate and insistent of all human needs. Yet we cannot force someone to love us. We cannot claim love as a human right. But the vision of society in which the alienation between man and man, man and woman would be overcome – perhaps the most persistent political vision there is – imagines a world where the love of others would be ours for the asking.

There are other needs, besides love, which test the limits of what politics can possibly offer. We are the only species with needs that exceed our grasp, the only species to ask questions about the purposes of our existence which our reason is unable to answer. Contemporary politics is largely silent about this need for metaphysical consolation and explanation, but, next to love, it is one of our strongest promptings and one which is utterly unreconciled to the limitations of our ignorance. Is there a secular politics capable of satisfying this need for ultimate meaning?

To raise these questions is to raise the possibility that there are human needs which escape the domain and competence of political action altogether. There may be a tragic gulf between what human beings need and what their collective wisdom is able to provide. Utopian thought is a dream of the redemption of human tragedy through politics. If politics is the art not merely of representing the needs of strangers but also of extending and increasing these needs, it must be careful not to conjure up the fierce and bitter emotions of disillusion. Disillusion with utopia is dangerous: it has often driven men and women to despair and reaction. The test of responsible political argument is to know which needs can be satisfied through politics and which cannot. Finding where this distinction lies is what this book is about.

If these are the questions, how are we to take them further? I am a historian, but the chapters which follow are not a history of need. I doubt in any case that a history of the word is possible, although it has been tried.[4] Need has been a central term in the language of Stoicism, classical tragedy, Augustinian Christianity, the Enlightenment discourse on the passions and the interests,

Marxism and psychoanalysis. Each of these languages is radically discontinuous with the others. Terms change meaning and conceptual position; the essential questions do not persist: they change in form with every language that poses them. The greatest of these breaks was between religious and secular languages of need. In the process, the very idea of spiritual need did not so much find a new guise as pass into silence.

Instead of a history, I have tried to write about the themes which concern me in the form in which they were raised in the languages of the past. I have tried to leave the rutted road of contemporary political philosophy altogether and trace my way back along the winding paths of ways of thinking which now seem strange to us: the language of tragedy, of Christian sin, of human passion.

I begin with what is probably the most profound examination of need as a human obligation: *King Lear*, and in particular the king's speech which begins 'O, reason not the need!' The play is built around the contrast between the social world, where what a man needs depends on what is due to his rank and station, and the natural world of the heath, where men's needs are those of the 'poor, bare, forked animal' we all are beneath our clothes. In moving from one world to the other, through madness and dispossession, Lear has something to teach us about the fragility of both natural and social obligation.

King Lear is also a play about blindness, in particular our blindness to our own needs. What we need, Lear discovers, we can barely admit; we learn what we need by suffering. We learn how much is enough by learning what it is like to have less than enough. Our education in need is a tragic passage from blindness to sight.

The play is also about the distinction beween those needs whose satisfaction we have a right to claim from others and those which we do not. Of these, Lear learns at a horrible cost, the first is love.

This dividing line is also central to the second way of thought examined in this book: Augustine's theology. The distinction between the City of God and the City of Men implies a distinction between needs of the body and needs of the spirit, between the secular goods which the politics of men can supply and the religious goods which only faith can provide. Augustine also distinguished between the freedom available to man in a secular polity – the freedom to choose – and the freedom of the redeemed: action freed by faith from doubt. Secular politics, he argued, can never deliver both freedom of action and certainty of will. In the City of Men, the citizen is free to choose among his desires, but he can never be certain that he has chosen what he needs. Recovering this ancient language of sin helps us to diagnose the particular loneliness and anguish of modern secular freedom.

The third chapter of the book is an attempt to trace some of the consequences of the Enlightenment's abandonment of a language of religious need, using the work of the greatest of eighteenth-century unbelievers, David Hume. The challenge of the commercial society taking shape around the philosophers was to understand how the competitive individuals of a market economy managed both to co-operate with each other and to find persuasive reasons for living. Hume's social philosophy is among the first to understand the order of modern civil society as a 'system of needs', to use Hegel's term, as an order maintained by each individual's dependence on strangers for the satisfaction of their needs.

Hume believed – and sought to demonstrate by the stoic manner of his own death – that secular man could live a persuasive and contented life in civil society entirely without religious or metaphysical consolation. The question of whether this is true, whether the needs we once called religious can perish without consequence, remains central to understanding the quality of modern man's happiness.

The social sciences which descend from the Enlightenment's science of man did more than secularize the language of need. In the process they diminished the tragic dimensions of human needing itself, once expressed in the religious yearning for ultimate certainty. What remained of the idea of human transcendence was an ironic doctrine of Prometheanism: man's blind needs for material things propel him towards the mastery of nature and in turn, without his knowing or intending it, towards the enlargement and transformation of his own needs. Promethean man creates progress, and re-creates himself in the blind spiral of his own needing.

Rousseau's revolt against this ironic doctrine of blind progress brought home to his contemporaries, as it does for us, the dimensions of tragedy in human needing which were suppressed in political economy's account of capitalist man. Rousseau's *Second Discourse on Inequality* rewrote the history of human needs as tragedy, as the story of how man had mastered nature only to enslave himself to the upward spiral of his own needs.

In his political thought – the subject of the final chapter of this book – Rousseau tried to define a utopia, a republic of virtue, which would redeem man's tragic history of need. His was a static republic which, by legislating against inequality and luxury, would try to stop the upward spiral of need that was the root of human envy and strife. His was the most sustained eighteenth-century attempt to vindicate a utopia in the emerging world of early capitalism, and it failed. In Adam Smith's *Wealth of Nations*, there is a ruthless demolition of the illusions of utopian economics, in particular the illusion that a republic could insulate itself from foreign luxury, the international market and the division of labour. This cold dose of realism has haunted the utopian project ever since: how can a society become master of its own needs within an open international economy? The domain of polity is the nation; the domain of economy, the world. How can a polity be sovereign over its economy in such conditions? If it shuts out the outside world and attempts, in the modern phrase, to 'build socialism in one country', it risks extinguishing the liberty of its subjects in a dictatorship over their needs; if it opens its doors, it risks the extinction of its experiment in virtue at the hands of international competition. With these dilemmas in the struggle for a politics which would make men and women in society the masters of their own needs, the book returns, in its conclusion, to the questions with which it began.

I · THE NATURAL AND THE SOCIAL

Thou art the thing itself;
unaccommodated man is no more
but such a poor, bare, forked animal
as thou art.

KING LEAR, III, iv

Questions about human needs are questions about human obligations. To ask what our needs are is to ask not just which of our desires are strongest and most urgent, but which of our desires give us an entitlement to the resources of others. This natural pairing of the idea of need with the idea of duty and obligation is what distinguishes need from desire. Need is bounded by the idea of the necessary or the essential. Desire is unbounded even by the idea of utility. It is possible to specify the duties which would follow from an obligation to meet someone's needs. But the duty would be boundless, and therefore meaningless, if it extended to a person's desires.

Need is a vernacular of justification, specifying the claims of necessity that those who lack may rightfully address to those who have. Without a language of need, and the language of right that derives from it, the human world would scarcely be human: between powerful and powerless only the law of hammer and anvil, master and slave would rule. The pathos of need, like the pathos of all purely verbal claims to the justice or mercy of another, is that need is powerless to enforce its right. It justifies an entitlement only if the powerful understand themselves to be obliged by it.

What is it then which binds those who have more than enough and those with less than enough in the ties of obligation? For most people, obligations are a matter of custom, habit and historical inheritance as much as a matter of explicit moral commitment. But might there not be something more than custom, habit and inheritance? Whatever the customs of a country, it would seem 'unnatural' for a father to deny his duty towards the needs of his children, unnatural for a daughter to refuse to give shelter to her homeless father. Beneath all these, there is nature: the natural feeling which ought to exist between father and children and more mysteriously between human beings as such.

The language of human needs is a basic way of speaking about this idea of a natural human identity. We want to know what we have in common with each other beneath the infinity of our differences. We want to know what it means to be human, and we want to know what that knowledge commits us to in terms of duty. What distinguishes the language of needs is its claim that human beings actually feel a common and shared identity in the basic fraternity of hunger, thirst, cold, exhaustion, loneliness or sexual passion. The possibility of human solidarity rests on this idea of natural human identity. A society in which strangers would feel common belonging and mutual responsibility to each other depends on trust, and trust reposes in turn on the idea that beneath difference there is identity.

Yet when one thinks about it, this is a puzzling idea. For who has ever met a pure and natural human being? We are always social beings, clothed in our skin, our class, income, our history, and as such, our obligations to each other are always based on difference. Ask me who I am responsible for, and I will tell you about my wife and child, my parents, my friends and relations, and my fellow citizens. My obligations are defined by what it means to be a citizen, a father, a husband, a son, in this culture, in this time and place. The role of pure human duty seems obscure. It is difference which seems to rule my duties, not identity.

Similarly, if you ask me what my needs are, I will tell you that I need the chance to understand and be understood, to love and be loved, to forgive and be forgiven, and the chance to create something which will outlast my life, and the chance to belong to a society whose purposes and commitments I share. But if you were to ask me what needs I have as a natural, as opposed to a social being, I would quickly find myself restricted to those of my body. I would abandon the rest as the work of my time and place, no less precious for all that, but not necessarily a universal human claim or entitlement. Yet even the natural identity of my body seems marked by social difference. The identity between such hunger as I have ever known and the hunger of the street people of Calcutta is a purely linguistic one. My common natural identity of need, therefore, is narrowed by the limits of my social experience here in this tiny zone of safety known as the developed world.

Why bother with the natural then, so long as the social tells us what we ought to do? The problem, of course, is that the social does not always tell us what to do. We may know what our obligations are to our families and friends and our fellow citizens, but what are our obligations to those strangers at our gates? Take one step outside our zone of safety – the developed world – and there they are, hands outstretched, gaunt, speechless or clamouring in the zone of danger. There is no claim of kith and kin to connect us together: there is only the indeterminate claim of one human being upon another.[1]

What these claims from strangers make so painfully clear is the asymmetry between natural and social obligation. The lives of a father, a daughter, a son are precious to us; the lives of strangers count for little. If we have the same needs, the same natural identity, this should not be so. Why does our natural identity count for so little, why does difference count for so much?

The natural identity of need helps one to understand why the new language of universal claims – the language of universal human rights – makes so little headway against the claims of racial, tribal and social difference. The needs we actually share we share with animals. What is common to us matters much less than what differentiates us. What makes life precious for us is difference, not identity. We do not prize our equality. We think of ourselves not as human beings first, but as sons, and daughters, fathers and mothers, tribesmen, and neighbours. It is this dense web of relations and the meanings which they give to life that satisfies the needs which really matter to us.

There is no deeper reflection on the claim of need, on the role of the natural and the social in the grounding of the claim, than *King Lear*.² It is a play that sets out to show us why we must take the needs of others on trust, by showing how murderous and pitiless a place the world can become without such trust. The claim of need makes the relation between the powerful and the powerless human, but the nightmare of the powerless is that one day they will make their claim and the powerful will demand a reason, one day the look of entreaty will be met with the unknowing stare of force. This is the nightmare which Lear begins to endure in Act II, Scene 4:

> *Goneril:*   Hear me, my lord:
> What need you five-and-twenty, ten, or five,
> To follow in a house where twice so many
> Have a command to tend you?
> *Regan:*   What need one?
> *Lear:*   O, reason not the need! Our basest beggars
> Are in the poorest thing superfluous.
> Allow not nature more than nature needs,
> Man's life is cheap as beast's. Thou art a lady;
> If only to go warm were gorgeous,
> • Why, nature needs not what thou gorgeous wear'st,
> Which scarcely keeps thee warm. But, for true need –
> You heavens, give me that patience, patience I need.

Kings in the fullness of their power do not have to speak the language of need. Theirs can be the pure and unjustified language of desire: 'Do it, for it is my wish.' Kings do not have to justify their desires. The most inconsequential of their whims has the force of a command.

All his life Lear had been addressed in the supplicating language of need. Now, for the first time, he must use the language himself. Its taste is bitter. He discovers that need may seem reason enough when spoken to the self alone, but when spoken to the pitiless and powerful, it must indeed be reasoned. His daughters' demand for reasons is so stinging an intimation of his new powerlessness that he cannot avow or accept it. He veers uncertainly between the usages of a king and the entreaties of a subject. Like a king, he says he has a claim that brooks no argument, and yet, like a subject, he is obliged to call his claim a need; thus he is entrained against his will to justify it, to offer reasons.

In what does the force of his claim reside? You are my daughters, he says, and a daughter does not reason her father's needs; to do so would be to deny the reality of familial obligation. To ask for reasons is not merely insulting or disobedient; it puts into question the plain meaning of family duty.

What Lear says he needs – a retinue of knights – counts as a need only within a given time and place, a given zone of safety guaranteed by a history of obligations and commitments. To call this need into question by the standards of some abstractly equal conception of what all humans might need is nonsensical. If all of us were to be judged by the standards of our common natural identity, Lear says, few of the needs we have in social life would survive examination: only those people prepared to go around like animals would escape censure. The social world, he insists, is a world of difference where each person's needs depend on their rank, position and history. Daughters who question a father's needs are doing much more than displaying ingratitude: they make their greed and pride the only standard of what shall pass as need in the world under their power.

Lear reasons not only as a father but also as a man. To reason any man's needs, he says, is to presume that he lacks the capacity to know his own mind. It was exactly this which his daughter Regan had just done:

> O, Sir, you are old;
> Nature in you stands on the very verge
> Of her confine. You should be rul'd and led
> By some discretion that discerns your state
> Better than you yourself.

Such is the revenge that youth takes for its years of tutelage. Fathers tell daughters what they need, whom they must marry, but when fathers begin to falter, daughters seize the reins and dictate the terms to age. The father is made child again.

The irony of these reversals is made more painful for Lear because it was the wilfulness of his initial generosity which convinced both Goneril and Regan that he had ceased to know his own mind. Alone on stage after the chilling love-auction of Act I, Scene 1, in which they, against all their expectations, receive half the kingdom each while the loved Cordelia is banished, Regan and Goneril reason shrewdly that their good fortune must signify their father's incipient dotage:

'Tis the infirmity of his age; yet he hath ever but slenderly known himself.

It is a recurrent theme of the play that there is a truth in the brutal simplicities of the merciless which the more complicated truth of the merciful is helpless to refute. The truth of the merciless – Goneril, Regan and Edmund – is that the fulcrum of family relations is power, not obligation. For them, it is power which is at issue in Lear's insistence on a retinue. A band of armed knights within their house but not under their command would threaten the sovereignty of their household. As Regan says:

How in one house
Should many people under two commands
Hold amity? 'Tis hard; almost impossible.

The issue they understand is command, not need: who shall rule in their house, not what is due their father. They realize clearly enough that a king dispossessed of his retinue will be nothing more than a child in their house.

The vision of the merciless does have a certain clarity. After all, *does* Lear really know what he needs? In their eyes, at least, his needs seem to be contradictory: to renounce the throne while keeping the name and equipage of a king; and to reside with his daughters yet rule in their house. And there may be a 'darker purpose' beneath even these contradictions: to set his rest upon the 'kind nursery' of Cordelia, to be a king and to be free of care, to be a father and to be a child again. To the merciless, these contradictions seem to signify only senility.

But contradictions cease to seem so strange when viewed with the eyes of pity. A tender heart would know how to be both mother and daughter to an old man. In a house ruled by love, the question of command would never arise – a man could be both master and servant, father and child. Only in a house without pity do needs seem irreconcilable. Power allows a man only one of two possibilities: to be either the father or the child, either the king or the slave, either the master or the servant. But the beseeching register in 'reason not the need' invokes a house where needs are not reasoned because love knows how to reconcile their antinomies.

The register of Lear's speech is beseeching rather than per-emptory because he has already begun the dolorous process of self-awakening. Where once he might have responded with out-rage to Regan's implicit questioning of his needs, Lear now replies querulously. The centre of his self is beginning to crack. We have already seen him battering his head with his fists and crying,

> O Lear, Lear, Lear!
> Beat at this gate, that let thy folly in
> And thy dear judgement out.

We have already heard him, in the midst of the Fool's frantic efforts to distract him, suddenly recall his banishment of Cordelia and moan in remorse, 'I did her wrong ...' If he now stands before his daughters beseeching them not to reason his needs, it is only after drinking the gall of his own self-deception. His claim now is not that men always *do* know their needs. It may even be true, he would now say, that others sometimes see us more clearly than we can see ourselves, that in our impetuosity towards others and our terror towards ourselves we can never fully encompass the contradictions in our own needing. But in a human world, love and pity must take needs on trust. Human beings must be trusted to know themselves, however imperfect we admit self-knowledge to be, for without trust, there is no limit to oppression. If the powerful do not trust the reasons of the poor, these reasons will never be reason enough. A rich man never lacks for arguments to deny the poor his charity. 'Basest beggars' can always be found to be 'in the poorest thing superfluous'. Whether on grounds of concealed wealth, idleness, or self-neglect, beggars can always be found wanting. The demand that the poor give reasons is the demand that they show themselves 'deserving'. But as the playwright had said elsewhere, if we were to give every person what they deserve, 'who would 'scape whipping?' (*Hamlet*, II, ii). The claim of need has nothing to do with deserving; it rests on people's necessity, not on their merit, on their poor common humanity, not on their capacity to evoke pathos.

Once the rich begin to demand reasons, once they cease to take claims on trust, Lear asks, what obligations will survive? Will the entreaty of utter starvation be reason enough for the hard-hearted? Why stop there? 'Man's life is cheap as beast's.'

There is method in Lear's consideration of a beggar's claims. Once already, in full view of his court, he had played the pauper's part, kneeling and whispering between clenched teeth:

> I am old;
> Age is unnecessary; on my knees I beg
> That you'll vouchsafe me raiment, bed and food.

In this grimly self-punishing attempt to shame his daughters, he bade them acknowledge that he ought not to be treated like a beggar. Now, in 'O, reason not the need!' he begins to realize that this is precisely how he is to be treated. The daughters will give him only what any old beggar needs – food, shelter and clothing; they will not give him his due – a retinue.

Let us contrast these claims. What a man needs he does not earn or deserve. He does not have to justify his entitlement, only the extent of his necessity. His entitlement inheres not in his person but in his humanity. The ground zero of human obligation is that this common humanity is reason enough for a claim on another's superfluity. This claim is strictly egalitarian: each is entitled to the necessities of life, no more, no less.

What a person is due, on the other hand, *is* what they deserve. These are the additional claims, above the floor of basic need, that people can make by virtue of their merit, station, rank in life. If basic need is what is necessary to man as a natural being, these additional claims are due him as a social being. If a man's need is what is necessary to his survival, his due is what is essential to his honour – to his self-regard, and to the regard in which he is held by others. A king is due a retinue; a father is due the respect of his daughters. If the claim of need is egalitarian, a man's due is not. A beggar is not due a retinue. To those who have, more is due. To those who have nothing, the minimum is enough.

The crux of Lear's demand for a retinue is that these two criteria, though conceptually distinct, can never in fact be separated in any fully human concept of obligation. What a man needs is his due, and what is his due, he needs. He needs not only raiment, bed and food, but such raiment, bed and food as is due his rank, his virtue, his history. Lear's daughters accept only what claims he makes as a poor, bare, forked animal, while denying what is due him as father and king. But Lear insists that to give him, and by implication *any* man, only what he needs as a poor, bare, forked animal is to dishonour him. True need, he cries, leaving the sentence unfinished because he cannot bear to say what ought to be left unsaid, is a man's due. What any man is due is his honour, and no man, he cries, should ever be made to beg for his honour.

This is a passionate defence of a paradox: that to treat men equally – only as men – is to deny them the respect due to their humanity. To give to each only according to his need, but not according to his due, is to diminish each to the poor equality of his natural being. To treat each person as a human being is to give to each according to their merit, rank, quality and deserving – that is, unequally. The contemptuous equality implicit in his daughters' giving – that they will allow him no more and no less than they would any impoverished claimant at their gate – enrages and dishonours him.

In today's world, our profoundest political conceptions of human dignity are paired with the idea of equality. But in Lear's world, in Shakespeare's world, human dignity reposed on difference: on rank, title, on the vestments and retinue of kingship. In such a conception, human beings had dignity in the faithful discharge of the duties of their station. For Shakespeare, the dimensions in which human beings were equal – the equality of the body, of suffering, of mortality – were not intrinsic elements of human dignity. To be sure, Lear defends a world in which each person would have enough, but he also defends a proposition much less familiar to modern ears: that dignity reposes in difference, not in equality.

Yet if treating people unequally – according to their due – is the only way to respect them as human beings, what inequalities are just? What distribution to the deserving will not, in its turn, dishonour the needy? These questions of justice do not yet occur to Lear. The hard questions about equality and justice are posed only to the dispossessed. For the moment, he takes his stand on what he is due as a king over and above what he might need as a man.

The worst dishonour of his situation is that he should have

had to say any of this in the first place. 'O, reason not the need!' is a passionate defence of tacit truths in human life. Unspoken common ground is the very stuff of human connection. Having been forced to give reasons for what ought to have been left unspoken, Lear knows that his daughters see before them just another anonymous beggar. The tacit ground between father and daughter has been sheared away by greed, revenge and power, the words put in place of the unspoken have only the meaning that power wishes them to have, and the trust which did not require speech has been replaced by the sufferance with which force condescends to weakness. The thought that the silent meanings which bind human beings together have been swept away by an act of his own doing is too much for the old man to bear:

> O fool, I shall go mad!

But there is more to Lear's madness than this. In the love-auction of Act I, Scene 1, Lear commands his daughters to declare their love before the whole court. The ritual is the more humiliating because it is superfluous. The daughters believe that nothing they say will make any difference: the old man has made up his mind, the lines on the map of his estate are already drawn, and the largest portion is already fixed on Cordelia. The cruel sovereignty of a king's desire demands one last display of its power: it commands another to declare the degree of its love.

This, of course, is the one thing that power can never command. Goneril and Regan's speeches are grovelling fakes. For love to speak true to power, it must prove its freedom of all fear. When Lear asks the one whom everyone knows loves him dearest only to say so at his command, truth bids her say

> Nothing.

And then,

> Unhappy that I am, I cannot heave
> My heart into my mouth; I love your majesty
> According to my bond; no more nor less.

There are needs whose satisfaction a bond can oblige: of such is the need for a retinue, and of such is obedience to a father's command. But the need for love is one that carries with it no implication of obligation. Lear's power deceives him into believing that his need is law over his daughter's love. But love is a gift, not a debt. Its injustice and its ingratitude are that it cannot be 'heaved into the mouth' on command. This is the truth that Cordelia, with all the ruthless self-righteousness of youth and some of her own father's wilfulness, bids him hear. Its defence admits of no compromise. Love that ceases to be sovereign in its promptings ceases to be love. Her husband to be, France, understands this well enough when he says in her defence:

> Love is not love
> When it is mingled with regards that stand
> Aloof from the entire point.

But who could be so blind as to miss 'the entire point'? Who actually believes that they can command the love of another person? To suppose that Lear actually believes he has the right to extract *authentic* declarations from his daughters is to suppose that kingship has taught him nothing about what power and the prospect of advantage do to a subject's avowals. As Stanley Cavell has suggested, it is more plausible to interpret the love-auction scene on the assumption that Lear does know the difference between authentic love and ritual performance.[3] He does not ask 'Which of you loves us most?' but only 'Which of you shall we say doth love us most?' He is apparently concerned with what is said rather than with what is felt. In any case, the division lines on his map are already drawn. Power is demanding obeisance to a will already resolved on its course.

Lear knows the difference between what he can command and

what he needs. What he asks of Cordelia is no different from what he asks of the others: in both cases, a formal exercise will suffice. For formal exercises do not require a symmetrical declaration on his part. They can be rewarded in the coinage of power, that is, in the grant of territory and dominion. A real declaration from the daughters, on the other hand, would require *him* to confess his love.

If this is what Lear intends, Cordelia's fault is not that she will not declare her love, but that she declares it all too plainly. Worse, her declaration reveals the ruthless exclusivity of his need for her. She says:

> Haply, when I shall wed,
> That lord whose hand must take my plight shall carry
> Half my love with him, half my care and duty.
> Sure I shall never marry like my sisters,
> To love my father all.

To talk of halves of love is no carping algebra of affection, but a daughter's defence of the autonomy of her desiring against a father who would have all. Lear wants a purely formal ritual occasion, but Cordelia wants a moment to speak the truth about family desire. The passionate 'Nothing' declares the intensity of her own love and the irreconcilable nature of his demand: what he wants of her would entail her sexual destruction.

It is not her ingratitude, then, that Lear cannot bear, but her knowledge of his need. Yet even here, at the edge of catastrophe, one could imagine another man stepping back, and admitting the daughter's truth. This would be hard enough even for a man learned in humility, but impossible for one blinded by power. In torment at her truthfulness, Lear chooses the path of disavowal:

> Here I disclaim all my paternal care,
> Propinquity and property of blood
> And as a stranger to my heart and me
> Hold thee from this for ever.

This impossible disavowal is yet another of power's ironic encounters with what it cannot command, even in itself. A daughter, Lear later admits, is a 'disease that's in my flesh', not a servant who can be banished. In some region of the mind, Lear knows this the instant the disavowal is out of his mouth. He turns in rage and anguish to Kent and says:

> I lov'd her most, and thought to set my rest
> On her kind nursery.

In the word 'nursery', need makes its intentions plain: to set his rest on her, as a man rests his head on a lover's lap, as a child rests in his mother's arms. For this only, for the impossible return to all beginning, would he be willing to relinquish power.

Lear's need for Cordelia is need in the cruellest meaning of the term. It is a lust that power is powerless to renounce, a compulsion that knows no law but its own prompting. The double impossibility of this need – either of achieving its satisfaction or of choking it down – is cruel enough for any father, but for a monarch who has never been thwarted it provokes the flight into madness.

When Lear rushes off into the storm, accompanied only by the fool and Kent, he crosses the divide between the social world and the no-man's-land beyond reason and obligation. In Shakespeare's time, this no-man's-land was very close, at the edge of the city and the village. It began where the line of enclosed fields ended, where the ambit of the parish constable and the magistrate trailed away, where the employer gave up the chase. The heath was the huge expanse of England beyond the reach of enclosing agriculture and the centralizing state, a realm of wild growth and darkness without patrols or police, king's highways or lights. It was the home of escapees from village order, paupers denied a parish settlement, vagrants escaping the oppression of wage labour, masterless men without land or trade of their own, madmen like Tom O'Bedlam, fugitives from justice and old people abandoned or thrown out of their families.[4] This world beyond custom and obligation exerted a deep hold on Shakespeare's imagination. Hamlet peers out at this dark world beyond the castle battlements; Macbeth goes in search of the three witches beyond the safety of his castle keep.

The heath is both a real place and a place in the mind. It is what the human world would be like if pity, duty and the customs of honour and due ceased to rule human behaviour. It is the realm of natural man, man beyond society, without clothes, retinue, pride and respect. But natural man has a terrible identity, Lear learns – the identity of life at degree zero, a hair's breadth from death. It is an equality of abjection that no man can endure.

In Lear's downward flight, by harrowing stages, reason is delivered out of madness, and sight out of blindness. Lear begins the voyage of self-abasement and self-recognition in an extremity of pride. Only a king would have dared rush out into the night on the heath to embrace desolation, to learn comradeship with the wolf and owl, to search out 'necessity's sharp pinch'. Those born into necessity, the Fool remarks, never search her out, and those used to nature's 'horrible pleasure' do not trouble themselves about her injustice. Only a king would see in the impersonal violence of a storm a judgement intended for a sovereign's head.

From this moment at the beginning of the storm, when madness produces a caricature of power in all its arrogant and self-justifying blindness, the downward progress to sight passes through distinct stages of dispossession. In the hovel, catching sight of the mad beggar Poor Tom (Edgar in disguise), Lear's wits 'begin to turn', as he says himself. He glimpses himself for the first time not as a king whom fate has marked off for retribution, but as a man suffering with others:

> How dost, my boy? Art cold?
> I am cold myself. Where is this straw, my fellow?
> The art of our necessities is strange,
> That can make vile things precious.

The art of our necessities makes precious our equality as needing beings. Lear's self-pity begins to give way to pity for another, yet his pity still keeps the distance of a king:

> Take physic, pomp;
> Expose thyself to feel what wretches feel,
> That thou mayst shake the superflux to them,
> And show the heavens more just.

There is also the same new pity, and also the same saving distance, in the blinded Gloucester's speech to the beggar who is in fact his own son:

> Here, take this purse, thou whom the heaven's plagues
> Have humbled to all strokes. That I am wretched
> Makes thee the happier. Heavens, deal so still!
> Let the superfluous and lust-dieted man
> That slaves your ordinance, that will not see
> Because he does not feel, feel your power quickly;
> So distribution should undo excess,
> And each man have enough.

From this, the pity that makes for reparation and distributive justice, the pity of a king, there is one more step down, to the pity of common nakedness, the final equality of basic need. In the inspiration of his madness, Lear takes this final step, surrendering any thought for what was once due a king. His speech breaks down from verse into snatches of common prose, bearing the starkest truth:

Is man no more than this? Consider him well. Thou owest the worm no silk, the beast no hide, the sheep no wool, the cat no perfume. Ha! here's three on's are sophisticated! Thou art the thing itself; unaccommodated man is no more but such a poor, bare, forked animal as thou art.

In the final discarding of the self-protecting pity of a king, Lear embraces the equality of need with what might almost be a mad kind of joy. He begins to tear at his clothes,

Off, off, you lendings! Come; unbutton here.

If only we could let nothing – our distancing pity, our sense of honour, our sense of due – stand in the way of our knowing how one we are with each other, Lear seems to say. One can imagine Lear suddenly mad with love for poor naked Tom. No claim of retinue now, no claim of due to separate himself from others: utter dispossession has taught him pity for the nakedness that is our only common possession.

Pity is a complex human emotion, mingling compassion and contempt. The mad king expresses these opposite registers – compassion for the essential wretchedness of natural man, and contempt for the pitiful identity all men ultimately share. The humanism of our day represents respect as an intrinsic right of all human beings: yet what exactly, Lear cruelly asks, is there to respect in a poor beggar covered with sores, raving and tearing at his clothes in a deserted hovel in a storm? What is there to respect in a mad tattered king, abandoned by retinue, by pomp, even by reason itself? What respect, Shakespeare would have us ask, is owed a human being as human being? It is one thing to answer this question in the zone of safety – in the castle, the family, the social world. There the humans we meet come clothed in difference, and the respect due to them is constituted by difference: by their wisdom, kindness, kingliness, natural authority, beauty, rank and stature. But what are we to answer in the zone of danger: in the no-man's-land of extremity, beyond family, beyond culture, beyond the safety of institutions which guarantee the respect we owe to difference?

On the heath, human beings have the body in common, and nothing else. King and beggar no longer share reason: they babble together like birds. In physical suffering alone are they equal, and in this alone are they the same.

Again, the humanism of our day believes that human beings have much more in common than this. Our needs are greater than the needs of our bodies. We are creatures of reason and speech, and it as creatures who, alone of all the species, can create and exchange meaning that we all have intrinsic needs for respect, understanding, love and trust.

These seem to be more generous and humane assumptions to make about human nature than the view that Shakespeare presents in his vision of the heath. Yet humane assumptions have unintended consequences. As soon as one enlarges the definition of the human, real human beings begin to be excluded: the Tom O'Bedlams of our time, the mad kings, the insane, the retarded, the deaf and dumb, the crippled and deranged. Those doctors and magistrates who have taken upon themselves the awesome business of deciding who is human – i.e. who is rational – have created a vast array of institutions designed to make Tom O'Bedlam and the mad king human again. The converse of the rational man has turned out to be man the disciplinarian, the man who takes upon himself the godly power of deciding who is in the sacred circle of reason and who is without. Enlarging the criterion of the human beyond the body has had the unexpected effect of legitimizing the despotism of reason over unreason.[5]

The mad king's recognition of the pitiful natural identity of the suffering body which he shares with Tom O'Bedlam makes no distinction between reason and unreason. It is our poor and weak flesh we share, and nothing else. But if this is so, what respect is due to it? What pity is owed to all forms of human suffering? Lear insists that the test of human respect is in life's hardest cases: not in one's neighbour, friend or relation, but the babbling stranger, the foul and incontinent inhabitant of the back wards of state hospitals, the mongol child. If poor unaccommodated man is no more than this, it is no wonder our pity conceals contempt.

Yet even from this moment of extremity, the stripping and discarding of superfluity which began on the heath must go further still. Men can be unequal in their needs, in their honour, in their possessions, but also in their rights to judge others. The king's ultimate inequality is that he is never judged. Even in madness, Lear had clung to his prerogative of judgement, as if to save himself from the final descent. In the hovel, he had acted out an insane ritual, arraigning a joint stool, making it represent one of his daughters and then passing thunderous judgement on her ingratitude, only to feel his righteousness ebb away under the scrutiny of three little dogs' eyes:

> The little dogs and all,
> Tray, Blanch, and Sweetheart, see, they bark at me.

What right of judgement does a man have whom even the dogs treat like a mangy beggar? Their barking pierces his madness and makes him see what he has become. His right to judge, he begins to understand, rested on a presumption of immunity from common bestiality. He begins to put his immunity aside:

> Thou rascal beadle, hold thy bloody hand.
> Why dost thou lash that whore? Strip thy own back;
> Thou hotly lusts to use her in that kind
> For which thou whip'st her.

He who had once inveighed against the secret incestuous wishes of others now confesses, 'None does offend, none, I say none', and as if to complete the unrobing of the judging king he begins pulling off his boots and asks blind Gloucester to help him.

Yet if the right of judgement can be thrown off, like a pair of boots, there are other things that cannot be renounced, however much a man might wish he could. There would be no tragedy in *King Lear* if it were only the story of one man's harrowing education in humility. Needing would not be tragic if we could learn to give up what we cannot get. But we are not animals: our needs and our realities are not made for each other.

Lear's suffering burns out of him his right of judgement and his self-protecting pity, but it cannot burn away the need for which the suffering has been endured. Desire can be renounced and wishes bleached away by the passage of time. But the tragedy of a need, in the sense in which Lear's feeling for Cordelia is a need, is that it can be neither renounced nor endured. In this impasse over the demands of a compulsion, he rushes this way and that in a maze of his own making, now avowing, now disavowing the lusts that torment him.

Who exactly is the 'simpering dame' he fixes in the sights of his rage? Who is it

> Whose face between her forks presageth snow,
> That minces virtue and does shake the head
> To hear of pleasure's name.

Who is it who receives the thrust of his raging diatribe against women in general?

> Down from the waist they are centaurs,
> Though women all above;
> But to the girdle do the gods inherit,
> Beneath is all the fiend's;
> There's hell, there's darkness, there's the sulphurous pit,
> Burning, scalding, stench, consumption, fie, fie.

If Cordelia is one of the targets of his fury, who is the other? Whose face, after all, 'presageth snow' but his? The most desperate of his strategies of disavowal is to transpose his own desires on to the body of the one he loves and then to rain down upon it the punishment he cannot bear to visit upon his own.

Even at this moment, so near the end of his course, he cannot bring himself to avow his love for anyone. When Gloucester, blinded for loyalty to him, approaches and tries to kiss his hand, Lear draws it away, and says,

> No, do thy worst, blind Cupid
> I'll not love.

Cupid's offering to Lear is Gloucester's bleeding eye sockets. But even her worst is not enough. He acknowledges the sightless man – 'I know thee well enough; thy name is Gloucester' – but he will not love. Instead, as he wryly says, 'I'll preach to thee.' Yet in the exultant self-absorption of his madness, there is a glimmering of tenderness in the advice he gives Gloucester:

> Thou must be patient; we came crying hither.
> Thou know'st the first time that we smell the air
> We waul and cry.

Lear's love lies buried in the word 'patience'. Some shortening of the range of its meanings has occurred so that we cannot immediately feel the force it had in Shakespeare's time. Modern patience is proverbially short. The word is no longer synonymous, as it was in Shakespeare's time, with 'long-suffering', with the calm abiding of the issue of time. In the King James version of the Gospel according to Saint Luke, for example, the disciples ask the Lord how long they are to endure the lapse of time before the second coming. With a candour they can hardly bear, Jesus tells them that the time will be long and their suffering will be great. There will be earthquakes, famines, pestilences, great signs from heaven and great persecution on earth before the hour is nigh. He makes patience the very core of their discipleship: 'In your patience, possess ye your souls' (Luke 22.19).

Our modern word has also lost its particular association with the endurance of pain. Only the medical 'patient' retains an ironic ghost of an association with suffering. It is as if an unintended consequence of our scientific victories over pain has been that we are less patient with the pain that remains, so that we think of it as an unnecessary shame, and resignation to its power ignobly passive. Shakespeare's patience was active: constancy in the face of affliction and a certain sardonic acceptance of the lessons that pain has to impart.

But again, if Lear could learn his own lesson, there would be no tragedy. Something in his own evocation to Gloucester of childhood, of wauling and crying, sets him off again on his unerring path to self-destruction. Just after he says, 'When we are born, we cry that are come to this great stage of fools', the old frenzy – to be Cordelia's child and lover – returns. With the deadly accuracy of a child's temper, he aims his blow at the sons-in-law, at the sons whom law has placed where he aches to be. The old rage, not the judging king's, but the infant's wild exterminating fury, overpowers him:

> And when I have stol'n upon these sons-in-law,
> Then kill, kill, kill, kill, kill, kill!

From this extremity of need, there cannot be any deliverance or saving patience. Madness at least permits him to speak his need, and when Cordelia finds him at last, it allows him to be a child in her arms. Cordelia speaks to her 'child-changed father' and takes him in her arms, but it is much too late for 'restoration to hang on her lips'.

When he finally does acknowledge her, their reconciliation is haunted by the double quality of his need. The child-changed father is both child and father, both the old man in harmless second childhood and the passionate lover. Hence the excitable brittleness in Lear's feverish evocations of the happiness they are never to know together. Like two birds in a cage, alone, shut off from the world, like 'God's spies' looking down in secret on the emptiness of human striving – all his images of their life in the future are unreal and impossible. An old man in second childhood could live with his daughter in the open: but the need which burns in Lear could only be satisfied in confinement. His exultation in their common imprisonment is not the 'patience' of an old and spent man, but the harsh triumph of a lover:

> He that parts us shall bring a brand from heaven
> And fire us hence like foxes.

Cordelia weeps. Does she know the impossibility of what he wants? Heedless, he cries,

> Wipe thine eyes;
> The goujeres shall devour them, flesh and fell,
> Ere they shall make us weep. We'll see 'em starv'd first.

If none of this is to be, if the slave must kill the daughter and part them eternally, the necessity inheres in the law of Oedipus. The need is forbidden, and it must be punished. Loss must be irrevocable: 'Never, never, never, never, never!'

When Edmund gives the officer in his retinue the order to hang Cordelia, the 'slave' slouches off to do his master's bidding saying under his breath:

> I cannot draw a cart nor eat dried oats;
> If it be man's work, I'll do it.

This is the human world; man's work is the murder of his kind, not like the wolf in a snarling frenzy at his enemy's throat, but passionless, under orders, like a cart-horse between the shafts. It is as much man's work as shutting the doors of the castle on an old man shivering and lost in a storm. As much man's work as blinding another in hatred of the sight of his loyalty.

Yet man's work is pity, too; think of the serving man who takes up his sword against his master rather than allow Gloucester's blinding to proceed. He cries out,

> I have serv'd you ever since I was a child;
> But better service have I never done you,
> Than now to bid you hold.

He pays for his pity with his life, but his sacrifice begins the process by which the retribution of evil is accomplished.

The strategy of the playwright is extreme. He shows us the worth of human pity by showing us what the world is like without it, shows us the horror of ingratitude to show us what gratitude should mean to us, shows us how little we need as beasts, to show us how much we need as men. We are like that. The allegiances that make the human world human must be beaten into our heads. We never know a thing till we have paid to know it, never know how much is enough until we have had much less than enough, never know what we need till we have been dispossessed. We must be blinded before we can see. Our education in the art of necessity cannot avoid tragedy.

If need is a tragic idea, if *King Lear* is a tragedy of need, it is because those feelings we call needs have a necessity which can drive us even to our own destruction. Desire does not have the force for tragedy: it has the cunning to bend around reality, to send its shoots and tendrils over the walls of the real. But need cannot bend, cannot defer, cannot wait. It has no patience. It is tragic because it submits neither to the will, nor to the real. We are not animals to sit out the storm, to adjust our means to our realities. We are the only creatures who rage at the injustice of our fate, who struggle against our needs and the fates they prescribe for us.

There is one thing more to say. The heath of Shakespeare's time is gone. The landlords fenced it, put it down in furrows and grass and set the masterless men to work upon it for wages. Lighted highways were pushed through its darkness, and the King's peace was spread like a seamless cover on the land. At night, the police patrol its wastes. The vagrants are in the shelters or the unemployment rolls. Old men whom their daughters abandon now get their pension and a home visitor.

But there is still a heath; it is the vast grey space of state confinement. On the wards of psychiatric hospitals, the attendants shovel gruel into the mouths of vacant or unwilling patients; in the dispensaries, the drug trays are prepared; on the catwalks of the prisons, dinner is slopped into tin trays and thrust into cells. Needs are met, but souls are dishonoured. Natural man – the 'poor, bare, forked animal' – is maintained; the social man wastes away.[6]

There is another heath just behind us – in our past. Think of the camps which dotted the flat plains of northern and eastern Europe just forty years ago, which still dot the blank spaces of Siberia. To these empty places, bounded on the map by barbed wire and railway lines, came fathers and daughters, mothers and sons, each one an individual with a place in cities they had left behind, with a history reaching deep into the roots of the European past. Each came to these places with what Lear called a 'retinue': the clothing, the suitcases, the bearing, the marks of honour and respect which made each of them specially who they were. In these rectangles of barbed wire, these individuals were stripped of the rings, suitcases, hair, glasses and clothing that made each of them a separate historical being. Under the pulverization of separation, suffering and torture, they were broken down into equal units of pure humanity. Ours is the first century to make an experiment on this scale: to take millions upon millions of social beings and to reduce each of them to that abstraction, never before seen in such quantity – natural man, the pure human being, the staring victim behind barbed wire, poor Tom, 'the thing itself'.

Think of the millions upon millions of hands outstretched to receive the milk from the pitchers, the cup of grain from sacks that come from the rich countries. Their states are unable to feed them; their tribes have been smashed by famine; they are on the heath. Like all the others enduring the fission of suffering, they have, at the very end, only one claim to make: Lear's claim, Tom's claim, that because they are human they deserve to live. This last claim, as Lear had to discover, is the weakest claim that people can make to each other: it is the claim addressed to anyone, and therefore to no one. When there is no family, no tribe, no state, no city to hear it, only the storm hears it.

Lear thought that our social duties, like the duty of father to daughter, must be built upon a natural human duty which every human being accepts. He thought, as many of us think, that our social duties to specific persons in this time and place – our duties as fathers, sons, daughters or citizens – build up in a pyramid that rests on the solid shared ground of natural duty. That is how it ought to be. Beneath the social there ought to be the natural. Beneath the duties that tie us to individuals, there ought to be a duty that ties us to all men and women whatever their relation to us. In fact, beneath the social, the historical, there is nothing at all.

When a Jew could no longer appeal to his fellow German as a neighbour, as a friend, as a relation, as a partner, as a fellow Jew even, when at the end, naked at the barbed wire, he could only appeal to the man with the whip as a fellow human being, then it was more than too late. When men confront each other as men, as abstract universals, one with power, the other with none, then man is certain to behave as a wolf to his own kind.

To bring justice to the heath, to protect the Tom O'Bedlams hurled into no-man's-land by war and persecution, there has arisen the doctrine of universal human rights and the struggle to make murderers and torturers respect the inviolability of human subjects.[7] If we all have the same needs, we all have the same rights.

Yet we recognize our mutual humanity in our differences, in our individuality, in our history, in the faithful discharge of our particular culture of obligations. There is no identity we can recognize in our universality. There is no such thing as love of the human race, only the love of this person for that, in this time and not in any other.

These abstract subjects created by our century of tyranny and terror cannot be protected by abstract doctrines of universal human needs and universal human rights, and not merely because these doctrines are words, and whips are things. The problem is not to defend universality, but to give these abstract individuals the chance to become real, historical individuals again, with the social relations and the power to protect themselves. The heath must be ploughed up, put under the sovereignty of a nation armed and capable of protecting its people. The people who have no homeland must be given one: they cannot depend on the uncertain and fitful protection of a world conscience defending them as examples of the universal abstraction Man. If nations cannot feed their people, they must seize the means to achieve autarky and self-sufficiency in the satisfaction of basic need within the inernational economy. Woe betide any man who depends on the abstract humanity of another for his food and protection. Woe betide any person who has no state, no family, no neighbour-hood, no community that can stand behind to enforce his claim of need. Lear learns too late that it is power and violence that rule the heath, not obligation.

2 · BODY AND SPIRIT

*It is yearning that makes
the heart deep.*

AUGUSTINE

Philosophers have called man the political animal, the language maker, the tool maker, the rational animal, even the laughing animal. To define man in this way is to define what it means to be human in terms of the best in us. And the worst? On the heath, where men have only their flesh in common, some men treat the flesh of their brothers as so much meat.

To define what it means to be human in terms of needs is to begin, neither with the best, nor with the worst, but only with the body and what it lacks. It is to define what we have in common, not by what we have, but by what we are missing. A language of human needs understands human beings as being naturally insufficient, incomplete, at the mercy of nature and of each other. It is an account that begins with what is absent.

This sense of what it is to be human has its origins in the religious idea of sin. In the Judeo-Christian tradition, human nature was treated not as a fact or as a bundle of potentialities, but as a problem. How, Jews and Christians have asked, is man's fate as a creature of need to be reconciled with the ideal of the goodness of God? Why is man condemned to scarcity, toil, suffering and death? Why is he a creature of need and not of plenitude, of lack, rather than fullness, of homelessness rather than belonging?

Genesis 3.9–19, the story of Adam's punishment, identifies man's fall in his desire to have more than he needs, in the hubris that would not be content with the fullness of Paradise. Every account of human beings as needing creatures since has had to return to Paradise, to the state of nature, to account for this tragic loss of plenitude. If human nature had been content with plenitude, it would have had no history, only the bliss of a permanent present. Instead, we ate from the tree of knowledge and were expelled from the garden. Our nature was forced, by our sin, to have a history, and the history of our needs has been tragic: the toil and suffering of Adam's curse.

Sometime during the years between the sack of Rome by the Goths in AD 410 and the Vandals' destruction of his own bishopric in the North African port of Hippo in 430, Augustine meditated upon the verses in Genesis and devoted a book to them in *The City of God*, his monumental defence of Christianity against the pagans.[1]

Augustine devoted his attention to one question above all: the nature of sexuality in Paradise. How did Adam and Eve manage to obey the divine commandment to increase and multiply, without themselves committing the sin of lust? The Manichean sect, whose doctrines troubled Augustine in his youth, maintained that evil was incarnated in human desire; the Platonists likewise believed that the good was present only in the spirit. To reflect upon sex in Paradise, therefore, was to define what attitude a Christian ought to take towards the desires of the body. Augustine believed that both the Platonist and Manichean positions did the wisdom of God an essential injustice. To suppose that our bodies are tainted by primal wickedness is to suppose that God could have created evil. Surely the flesh is 'good in its own kind': Augustine sought to find a welcome in Christian doctrine for the pleasure of the marriage bed. But neither body nor spirit is a self-sufficient principle of good. It was in the unity of body and spirit in obedience to the commandment of God that Adam and Eve knew the serene happiness of Eden. In the garden, will and desire were in utter agreement. The marriage in Paradise 'would not have known this opposition, this resistance, this tussle between lust and will, or at least this contrast between the insatiability of lust and the self-sufficiency of the will'. In the sexual encounters of Paradise, 'the man would have sowed his seed and the woman would have conceived the child when their sexual organs had been aroused by the will, at the appropriate time and in the necessary degree'. Eve's womb would have opened by 'a natural impulse' to receive the seed, and when the time was ripe, it would have opened again to deliver itself of child. Because the two were one flesh and their will and their desire were one, there would have been no lust. There would have been no violence, no tearing of flesh, no travail in consummation or in birth. There would have been no shame in nakedness, no disgust in the body, no remorse in the soul, because body and soul would have been at one in obedience to God's command. In Paradise there would have been only the silent conjugation of wills between two creatures made of one flesh. No gulf of gender, no otherness of male and female. All this in a world beyond hunger, thirst, illness, exhaustion, pain and death. All this in a world perpetually ablaze with the love of God.

This account of Paradise lost is the first vision of transcendence we possess in our tradition. Standing as they do at the very beginning of Western culture, these verses from Genesis tell us something about ourselves: we have never been resigned or reconciled to what we are. Unlike any other species, what we yearn for, what we need, is beyond the limit of what we actually are. What we are, we long to transcend. That is the meaning of the glimpse of Paradise at the beginning of our culture. What we have become since the expulsion from the Garden is a fact, but it is also a problem, a fate we can hardly bear to endure:

For the flesh lusteth against the spirit and the spirit against the flesh: and these are contrary the one to the other. So that ye cannot do the things that ye would (Galatians 5.17).

What we will and what we desire are at enmity. Between the will to do the good and the act falls the shadow.

This opposition between will and desire, between spirit and

flesh, was central to the drama of Augustine's own conversion. In the garden of the little house outside Milan where his conversion was accomplished, Augustine knew the full torment of being unable to will belief:

I tore my hair and hammered my forehead with my fists; I locked my fingers and hugged my knees; and I did all this because I made an act of will to do it . . . . Yet I did not do that one thing which I should have been far, far better pleased to do than all the rest.[2]

At that moment and ever after, Augustine sought to understand why God had seen fit to divide human will and desire in this way. There was, it seemed, a division in the will itself, a natural will to do the good and a resistant will that chooses evil. This was the 'deep shadow', Augustine said, that had been cast over all the sons of Adam. It was this shadow's first coming which the verses in Genesis explained.

We can begin to understand now why Augustine devoted so much thought to the problem of sex in Paradise. Men in the earthly City, as he knew from his own experience of marriage, value nothing so highly as the extinction of self in sexual pleasure. The sentries of the intellect are disarmed; the body seems to fill the soul itself and, for an instant, both the divide within the self and between self and other are overcome.[3] If human estrangement is ever transcended in earthly life, it is overcome in sexual fulfilment. How important then for a Christian philosopher to show that this instant is but a diminished taste of the happiness we once effortlessly possessed, and which we can now recover only by faith in the mysteries of Grace. He sought, in other words, to track our alienation down to that refuge from which men of the earthly City believed they had shut it out.

Augustine insisted that our inner division manifests itself even in the 'sickness' of our sexual desire. Sometimes our sexual impulses force their commands upon our unwilling wills; sometimes they abandon the will, strangely refusing its call: 'Desire cools off in the body while it is at boiling heat in the mind.' The disobedience of the flesh, Augustine wrote, is God's punishment for man's disobedience in the Garden. It is not the corruptible flesh that makes the soul sinful; it is the sinful soul that makes the flesh corruptible.[4] Because we desired to know good and evil, we are fated ever after to know our bodies only as evil: to be ashamed of our nakedness, to seek covering, and to understand the good as the unremitting struggle of will against natural desire. The pagan Stoics glorified this struggle as a means to man's realization of human potential, but Christians know the tragedy of the struggle for what it is. There will never be, as the Stoics promised, a serene state of *apatheia* beyond yearning and striving in this life. Stoic self-command will never be anything else than 'coercion and struggle', a condition of guilt rather than a state of health.[5]

For Augustine it was a sign of God's pity that the Son he sent to live among men took it upon himself to suffer every temptation thrown up by the alienation between will and desire. When Jesus was fasting in the desert for forty days and forty nights, the tempter came to him and taunted him: 'If thou be the son of God, command that these stones be made bread.' Jesus replied with words which became the foundation of the Christian anthropology of human nature: 'It is written, Man shall not live by bread alone, but by every word that proceedeth out of the mouth of God' (Matthew 4.4). He told the poor and hungry people who came to hear him preach that God knew they had need of food and drink and clothing: they should first seek the kingdom of God, and all these secular hungers would be nourished (Matthew 6.33). For Christians the tragedy of need is that human beings do not naturally 'hunger and thirst after righteousness' as they hunger for food. Augustine knew the bitter truth of this from his own life. As he said when describing the young student he had once been, arriving in Carthage from the dusty provincial town of Thagaste to study oratory and to make his career in Africa's first city:

Although my real need was for you, my God, who are the food of the soul, I was not aware of this hunger. I felt no need for the food that does not perish, not because I had my fill of it, but because the more I was starved of it, the less palatable it seemed. Because of this, my soul felt sick.[6]

When Christians speak of the hunger for God, therefore, they are expressing a longing to know him in every particle of their being as certainly as they know the cravings of their bodies. The human dilemma after the Fall is that we have been delivered up to the determinations of our own will as to what is good and evil and yet we can never know, with certainty, that we have chosen correctly. How then are we to use the gift of our freedom? How are we to know, in other words, that what we want is what we need?

In his incomparable biography of Saint Augustine, Peter Brown draws our attention to the distinction Augustine made between two kinds of freedom: the freedom to make choices, and the freedom which comes from knowing that the choice one has made is the correct one.[7] Our first freedom, the freedom to choose, Augustine believed intrinsic to unredeemed human nature. Like the Stoics, he located our capacity for freedom in the ability of our will to choose between need and desire, to resist the claims of passion with the claims of virtuous and rational intention. For Augustine, as for the Stoics, need is a category of judgement and will, not a category of inclination and instinct. It is also explicitly individualistic: a criterion of personal judgement to be used in resisting the tide of others' desire. Augustine would have agreed with Seneca, 'Nature's wants are small, while those of opinion are limitless', and with Epicurus, 'If you shape your life according to nature, you will never be poor; if according to people's opinions, you will never be rich.'[8]

Unlike the Stoics, however, Augustine insisted that unredeemed reason can never know its choices to be right or natural. That second freedom is the gift of Grace alone. In the sermons on the Gospel according to Saint John, written at the end of his life, Augustine spoke of this second freedom as a state in which the soul would be as certain of the presence of Grace and of the necessity of the godly life, as the body is certain of the presence of immense pleasure. But who, he asked, could possibly know what he was talking about?

Give me a man in love; he knows what I mean. Give me one who yearns; give me one who is hungry; give me one far away in this desert, who is thirsty and sighs for the spring of the eternal country. Give me that sort of man; he knows what I mean. But if I speak to a cold man, he just does not know what I am talking about.[9]

This is one of the moments in which Christian language shows up our modern ideals of a good society. The only freedom which has a claim on modern attention is the first of Augustine's freedoms: the freedom to choose. We seem to have neglected the second: the freedom of action which comes from knowledge that one has chosen rightly. We have sought both as a private and as a political goal to expand our range of choices, all the time assuming that individuals will know what to choose if they are free to do so. We have assumed that freedom is a problem of external constraints: give everyone enough income and sufficient rights, and they will be free to act in accordance with their choices. But what if it were the case, as Augustine insists, that freedom is a tainted good unless choosing is accompanied by a sense of certainty? What point, what happiness, is there in freedom if we can never know whether we have chosen rightly? In the Augustinian discourse, this blessed certainty is a gift of Grace. Unredeemed man's choice between need and desire is bound to be blind, contingent, haunted by remorse and second thoughts.

Since modern political reason cannot begin from an assumption of Grace, how can we imagine a purely human solution to the problem of our second and most precious kind of freedom? How can we create a world in which most people will not only be free to choose but will know how to choose? Freedom and happiness can accompany each other only when individuals know that they have used their freedom rightly. What society could ever deliver this gift of Grace? Merely to ask this is to show how daunting, how utopian is the vision of a society of individuals both free and happy.

It has been a recurrent dream of the Western political imagination to fashion a form of society that would so wrap the individual in the fraternity of his fellows that his choices would unerringly reconcile private and public interest, the claims of self and the other, in decisions that the choosing self would know were right. This was the utopia of More, Rousseau and Marx: each understood that freedom and happiness could be reconciled only if individual choice were always anchored in fraternity. But then what is left of freedom if choice is invariably guided by the collective wisdom of the brothers, the citizens, the comrades?

In the human world, Augustine believed, there is no social arrangement that can guarantee anything more than a first freedom, with no necessary connection to happiness, a freedom estranged from the possibility of certainty, a lonely freedom. Individuals must choose, and they cannot be sure they have chosen wisely. They yearn for a second freedom, and the happiness that comes from certainty; they long for a utopia that will relieve them of the lonely burden of private judgement. But the escape from the first freedom into a utopia that promises the second is a leap into despotism; it is the choice to shake off the loneliness of private choice by embracing the chains of the happy slave. That choice and its temptations can be resisted only by minds convinced that there are some needs, some yearnings which this world cannot satisfy: in other words, that there is no secular equivalent to the state of Grace.

So many roads of devotion start their journey from Saint Paul and Augustine and their meditation upon the meaning of human freedom after the Fall, that I shall try to follow only one path into the Middle Ages and beyond. Consider the painting at the front of this book. It is called the Haywain, painted by the Flemish artist Hieronymus Bosch sometime in the 1490s in the small cathedral town of Hertogenbosch in Brabant. It was seized by the Spaniards during their occupation of the Netherlands, and hung on the gloomy walls of Philip II's Escorial in the next century. It has remained in Spain ever since and now hangs in the Prado in Madrid.

The Haywain itself is the central panel of a triptych, framed on the left by a panel depicting the causes of human sin, the Temptation and the Expulsion from the Garden, and framed on the right by sin's consequences, the horrors of eternal damnation. The central panel, therefore, can be interpreted as an allegory on the vanity of human wishes, in the form of a play on the theme of Christian life as a pilgrimage. Instead of following the Cross or some holy relic, the throng, which includes all sorts and conditions of men from beggars to kings, from impoverished priests to the Pope himself, is following in idolatrous attendance upon a cart filled to bursting with straw. As many medieval feast days and holy processions must themselves have been, this one is a scene of carnal rapacity: bodies clawing at each other, hands clutching at the straw, figures falling under the wheels of the juggernaut as it passes, two old beggars swinging at each other with their crutches, a villain holding a knife to a man's throat. No one seems to have wrested any hay for himself except the corpulent abbot at the bottom of the picture who watches with rotund complacency as nuns stuff his stack with the booty. The lordly figures on horseback and the frenzied crowd pay not the slightest attention to the fact that the haywain is being pulled downwards into the earth by a team of monstrous creatures with the heads of fishes, reptiles and foxes and the bodies of men.

The allegory would have been obvious to a Dutch peasant of the time at a glance. Its subject is the peasant proverb, 'All the world's a haystack, each man takes what he can snatch.' It also plays on the meaning of the peasant expression that when a person is making a fool of himself, he is grabbing at the hay, that his head is filled with straw.[10] This then is the first text with which to decipher the picture's meaning: the sardonic discourse of the poor on a scramble they always lose.

The second text for the deciphering of the allegory, so the scholars tell us, is indicated by the presence among the throng just beneath the figures on horseback of the sad-eyed prophet Isaiah. 'All flesh is grass, the grass withereth, but the word of our God shall stand for ever' (Isaiah 40.6–8).

The prophet exhorts the passing multitude, but in the sadness of his eyes we see that he knows his words have gone unheard. Only one figure in the painting struggles to do the prophet's bidding. In the centre of the picture a poor tonsured priest struggles to separate two fighting figures so bent on each other's destruction that they seem unaware that they are both about to be crushed beneath the wheels of the hay-cart.

In the twin figures of the poor parish priest and the sad-eyed prophet, we can perhaps get our first glimpse of the painter's mysterious moral place in his work. We know that Bosch was a prominent member of a confraternity of devout and wealthy laymen in his home town, the Brotherhood of Our Lady, and that some of his most deeply mysterious paintings were commissioned by the confraternity as expressions of its central beliefs. These brotherhoods, which dotted the towns of northern Europe in the century prior to the Reformation, attempted to reform the devotional life of the laity on monastic lines in the face of the worldliness and corruption of the Church. Small wonder then that the corpulent prelate in the bottom right of the picture seems to catch the full force of the painter's pious anger.[11]

The key inspirational text of these brotherhoods was Thomas

à Kempis's *Imitation of Christ*, composed in a Dutch monastery in the 1420s. It counselled believers to 'keep yourself a stranger and a pilgrim upon the earth, to whom the affairs of the world are of no concern.'[12] In the ideal of Christian pilgrimage, need served as a criterion for winnowing out desire, for willing that estrangement to earthly things which was essential to the achievement of a pilgrim's holy goals. Yet the line between need and desire was subtle and easily transgressed. Had not Saint Augustine himself confessed, 'Who is he, O Lord, who is not somewhat transported beyond the limits of necessity' in ascetic observance?[13]

How was the line of need to be drawn for the pious layman? Was he to follow the example of the heroes of asceticism, the hermits like Saint Anthony of Egypt who pushed the neglect of need to the extremes of masochism? Anthony was the painter's patron saint, yet how could his life be the standard for a man living in the modern world of a prosperous north European town? Church authorities since Augustine himself had condemned the dreadful pleasure of self-mortification. For the devout laymen of Bosch's confraternities, the *devotio moderna* of à Kempis and other writers provided precisely that *via media* between Saint Anthony's path and the path of worldly temptation, a regimen consistent with the ancient priority 'Seek ye first', and yet also adapted to the requirements of men who loved their wives, their families and, within limits, their possessions. Yet it was an uneasy truce with the things of this world. À Kempis remarked, almost mournfully, that if men could only be freed of their need for food, drink or rest, they would be free to praise God without ceasing; they would be fed by the 'spiritual feasts of the soul'. Men, he counselled, must remain exiles even from their own inner promptings.

If we look again at the Haywain with the eyes of one of à Kempis's devout lay brothers, we can see that its very colours are ablaze with anger at the blindness which mistakes vain desires for true needs, at the voracity and greed that turn men into wolves. Bosch's denunciation extended not only to the material things of which hay was the symbol, but to the delusions of love as well. Atop the haywain sit a respectable couple, the man playing the lute, the beloved listening both to the strains of the lute and to the devil's music just to her left. This couple is more decorous than the obviously carnal couple in the bushes behind them, but both are compassed within Bosch's condemnation.

Thus far the painting can be interpreted as a pictorial homily on folly, inscribed with all the certainties of the elect. Yet there is an additional presence which deepens the mystery and heightens the tension of its moral message. Above the priests and kings, the rich men and poor clawing at each other, stands a tiny figure in the clouds. His compositional insignificance cannot be accidental: he is diminished by the scene of folly, dwarfed by the monstrous procession. He merely watches, with hands outstretched in what might be taken as a gesture of either supplication or pity. All below disregard him.

This is the third text inscribed beneath the painting's luminous surface: the silent judgement of God. The peasant's sardonic wisdom, the warnings of Isaiah and the judging anger of a devout layman are all turned into mystery by this tiny figure, by our knowledge that this monstrous procession has passed through a world suffused with the serene golden light of his Grace.

If Bosch's own intentions were not now lost by time or at least hidden in his hermetic code of meanings, we might confidently say that the painting is both a discourse on the vanity of human wishes and also a reflection on the mystery of human free will. The tiny figure may be there to tell us that we have been left to choose our follies, and that we are responsible for all that has happened – the banishment from the Garden and our unheeding procession to hell. If this is so, if the painting is a learned man's reflection on the Augustinian doctrine of the Christian will, we are still in the dark as to Bosch's attitude towards this most difficult of mysteries. We might want to assume that a devout medieval laymen would not have any of our doubts as to how this mystery is to be understood.

Yet there is something about his work which allows us to imagine, even if we cannot prove, that Bosch's inspiration was guided as much by doubt as by faith, or perhaps by faith's meditation upon doubt. Consider, for example, the work which Bosch painted on the back of the left and right panels of the Haywain triptych and which, when the triptych is closed, come together to form one picture. Like the Haywain, this picture plays on the meaning of pilgrimage and has been taken to represent the one godly man who escaped the infernal scene shown on the other side.

The godly man is presented as a weary and threadbare tradesman with a pack on his back; he stands before a rickety bridge and looks back anxiously along the meandering path he has taken. A cur with tiny white teeth is nipping at his heels, and the weary traveller is keeping him at bay with his staff. He is beset with danger and temptation on all sides. In the fields behind him another traveller has been set upon by thieves who have tied him to a tree and are pillaging his pack. The story of the good Samaritan offers the traveller a clear injunction to intervene, but he hesitates, frightened and confused. In front of him, on the left, a peasant plays the siren song of the bagpipes while a labouring woman dances lewdly with a mower with a sickle in his hand. Again the traveller hesitates, torn between pleasure and the Christian road ahead. It is a daunting portrayal of the demands of the path of Christian righteousness, made all the more forlorn because we are not given to see what it is that the traveller has left behind him.

A decade later, when Bosch re-worked the figure in a new painting, he did show the scene the wayfarer had left behind. It is a dilapidated tavern in whose doorway stands a serving woman surrendering to the rough attentions of a traveller, while in another window a woman gazes enticingly at the wayfarer himself.

A shutter is hanging from one of its hinges; underwear is draped over an upstairs window sill; in the yard, where sows grunt over their feed and a cock stands astride a dung-hill, a drunken man relieves himself unsteadily against a wall. Ahead of the traveller stretch the lonesome dunes of the North Sea coast. He stands poised between the unknown road of pilgrimage and the unmistakable pleasures of the tavern.

À Kempis counselled his readers to keep themselves in exile from their own bodies, but he himself confessed that he had never found anyone, however religious or devout, 'who did not sometimes experience withdrawal of grace or feel a lessening of devotion'. The flesh, he said grimly, was never quite dead. Bosch's wayfarer can be interpreted as a representation of the austere difficulties of pilgrimage as the *Imitation of Christ* described them, and perhaps as Bosch himself had known them. Some scholars have argued that the wayfarer is in fact a self-portrait of the artist, as is the careworn face of the humble Christian who bears the wounded Saint Anthony on his back in Bosch's painting of the saint's temptation.[14] There is also a strange autobiographical blasphemy, perhaps, in the second way-farer painting: the sign hanging over the doorway of the dilapidated tavern/brothel depicts a swan, the sacred emblem of Bosch's confraternity, and its ritual dish on the occasion of its banquet. If a private joke is intended, it is another indication of the way his art manages to encompass both blasphemy and belief in an inscrutable personal synthesis.

The tension and anguish in this synthesis are also revealed in an absence in the wayfarer paintings. In neither of them is there any watching God. The only sight to greet the wayfarer if he cast his eyes heavenwards in search of guidance would be the unblinking eyes of an owl in the treetops. In medieval iconography, the owl was a symbol of heresy and religious delusion. The mystery of Bosch's private belief is held fixed and unknowable in the owl's glassy gaze.

Some scholars have argued that beneath their tonsured severity Bosch's confraternity was actually an Adamite free-love sect. Bosch's most extraordinary painting, the Garden of Earthly Delights, could then be decoded as a hermetic *ars amandi*, as a vision of the sinless joys of the body that await man's restoration to Paradise.[15] There is no doubt that Paradise and Saint Augustine's account of it haunted the Christian imagination, and that Bosch's Garden of Earthly Delights is a representation of the human reconciliation of body and spirit, will and desire, as described in Augustine's meditation and the verses of Genesis. The question is whether Bosch actually believed that it was a Paradise which could be regained in this life.

There were secret medieval sects which sought to approach the pinnacles of spiritual ecstasy through the rites of free love, under the guiding instruction of a master in the *ars amandi*. We have no way of knowing whether Bosch belonged to one of them, but the question is secondary. No one could have painted the huge strawberries on which the naked and guiltless lovers gorge themselves in the Garden of Earthly Delights who had not himself known the ache of earthly desire. No one could have represented the lovers enclosed in the still peace of their crystal sphere who had not cast his imagination into the vision of Paradise in Genesis. Bosch's work is of course individual to himself, and perhaps even to the mysteries of a sect in a small medieval Brabant town, but its most fundamental source is the primal Christian longing for the reconciliation of flesh and spirit, self and other, beyond the frontier of guilt and shame.

Bosch's paintings capture all the tragic depth of this yearning. No more tormenting doubt could be addressed to the proposition that life had meaning only as a pilgrimage towards the reconciliation of flesh and spirit in the afterlife than the pungent persuasiveness of pleasure in this life. Bosch's paintings are an inquisition of the Providence that sets men to such a cruel service. If life is supposed to be a pilgrimage in which we, like the wayfarer, should neither tarry at the inn nor accumulate more than we can carry on our backs, why then are the strawberries so sweet, why then is the smiling woman in the window gifted with such infernal power in her beckoning? And why does God keep silent in the clouds, giving us no more guidance in the choices of our freedom than an owl's stare from the treetops? None of the gods invented by human reason can answer questions such as these.

Bosch's reflection centred on a problem intrinsic to all Christian metaphysics: whether spiritual need forms part of the natural yearnings of unredeemed human nature. There had always been two polar positions on the issue – the Pelagian and the Augustinian. The heresy of Pelagius, a late-fourth-century Roman Briton, maintains that human nature was created with a capacity to redeem itself, to merit salvation and Grace by acts of its own will, and that human evil is an encrustation of habit and history which devout men could cleanse away by ascetic practice. From the Augustinian point of view, the Pelagian heresy blasphemously exalts the capacities of human will and reason. Augustine insisted, with Saint Paul as his authority, that men forfeited the capacity to earn their salvation as a result of the Fall. So far from having any natural inclination to God, Augustine believed from his own spiritual travail that man's needs, the natural in man, are the chief marks of his corruption. To naturalize religious inclination as an intrinsic human need is to erode the necessity of utter submission to God; it encourages sinners to claim Grace as a right, and not to surrender to His inscrutable will.[16]

The medieval Thomist position sought to tread a subtle path between the heresy of treating human evil as a mere encrustation of habit, and the fatalistic doctrine that man can do nothing whatever to secure his own salvation. Aquinas accepted that man's desires were 'wounded' by the Fall, turned away from the natural inclination to the good they once possessed in the Garden. Yet men remain distinct as a species in the degree to which 'the power of desire is naturally ruled by reason'.[17] By rational mastery of desire according to the demands of a godly life, men can seek to attain the good for which they naturally yearn. He maintained that mankind yearns for a good it cannot attain in human life itself: the healing of its essential wound, the gulf between spirit and flesh. This reconciliation is the destination of the species:

Complete contentment there cannot be unless natural desire is wholly fulfilled. Everything craves what belongs to its nature, and therefore desires its parts to be re-united. Since the human soul is united by nature to the body there is within it a natural appetite for that union. The will could find no perfect rest until the soul and body are joined again. This is the resurrection of man from the dead.[18]

For Augustinians, this subtle scholastic attempt to naturalize the yearning for human wholeness as the immanent teleology of human desire makes too many concessions to human wickedness. Men can only become capable of hungering in that way if they vanquish their impetuous natures and put themselves entirely in the hands of their Creator. Then they might be suffused with that blessed sense of fate and certainty, beyond reason and will, which the metaphor of spiritual hunger describes. Only then, in the state of Grace, might they know true happiness beyond need.

This fullness can be evoked in the meagre language of physical satisfaction only because it shares with eating and drinking the characteristic of unmistakable sensation. Yet unlike physical need, which must be in language to be felt and known, it is ineffably beyond words. Did not the prophet write, 'The eye has not seen, nor the ear heard, nor has it entered in the heart of man the things which God hath prepared for them that love him'?

Erasmus of Rotterdam, a near contemporary of Bosch's, brought up like him in the pious lay confraternity of Hertogenbosch and other centres of *devotio moderna* in the 1480s, concluded his *Praise of Folly* with a famous evocation of Christian ecstasy. It is a state of pleasure, he wrote, so intense that it 'surpasses all corporeal pleasures even where they are combined into one vast pleasure'. Those who have experienced its force he said, will seem insane to those who have not:

They will speak in a manner that is not quite correct, nor in the ordinary manner but with meaningless sounds. Their facial expressions change from joy to sorrow, they weep and laugh, and, in short, are outside themselves. When they return to themselves, they admit they have no knowledge of where they have been, whether in body or out of it, whether waking or sleeping. They have no memory of what they heard or saw or did, as though in a dream, though this they do know, that they were most happy in this ecstatic state. They regret this return to their senses and prefer nothing more than going back to this state of madness. And this is but a small sampling of the future happiness.[19]

Saint Paul had written, 'But the natural man receiveth not the things of the spirit of God: for they are foolishness unto him: neither can he know them, because they are spiritually discerned' (1 Corinthians 2.14). What is encompassed here in Paul's condemnation is both the rational God of reasoners, the God of human theology whose attributes and justice are numbered and accounted for in the pitiful insufficiency of human calculation, and also the sober calculus of pleasure of natural man. The language of Christian ecstasy which derives from Paul insists on the radical insufficiency of the natural human conception of our own alienation. We have literally no idea of what we need to overcome the gulf of alienation in our nature. We must be pitched into the blind ecstasy of Christian fulfilment to know anything of the Paradise we once enjoyed within ourselves. Bosch's Garden is what awaits us beyond the limit of what we so miserably are.

In the Augustinian discourse, therefore, the certainty of Grace is delivered to men not in their reason but in violent certitudes of the body. When that most brilliant and troubled of seventeenth-century Augustinians, Blaise Pascal, was granted a moment of religious certainty, it came not in the language of rational proof – in the Cartesian demonstration or mathematical syllogism which one would have expected God to use when speaking to one of the inventors of the calculus – but in the language of fire, burning his senses as hotly as hunger. The piece of parchment that he sewed into his robe and kept about his person until his death recorded that 'In the year of Grace, 1654, Monday 23 November, from about half past ten in the evening till half past midnight', he had been consumed by God's fire. The God who came to him in all the certainties of the body was not the 'God of philosophers and scholars' but the God of Abraham, Isaac and Jacob, not the God of rational argument but the God of ancient and simple faith.[20]

But if men can only know God with certainty when he speaks as plainly to their souls as hunger speaks to their bodies, as fire breathes on their skin, why do so few of us ever live to see our night of fire? A rational mind might suppose that God could bind his flock to him for ever if he made faith speak as loudly and clearly to the soul as hunger speaks to the body. Yet he manifestly does not, and this was, for Jansenists like Pascal, a poignant mystery.[21]

The Augustinian sensibility that Pascal shared with Bosch was horrified by the fact that the ordinary people around them seemed to be in no evident need of the kind of existential and metaphysical certainties they yearned for. With a kind of terror, they watched their fellow men crowding after the Haywain without so much as a glance at the abyss ahead. The perplexing fact about lives given over to the satisfaction of ordinary material needs is that they seem capable of generating their own self-validation. The simplest pleasure has the capacity to produce more genuine assurance of the worth of existence than many a tortured chain of reasoning about God's ultimate purpose for mankind. The terror of life, for Augustinians, was that it is so inexplicably endurable. And death? Pascal remarked that the same man who spends so many days and nights in fury and despair at the prospect of losing some petty office hardly ever bothers to think about the prospect of his eventual extinction. A life spent in the pursuit of need is an upward spiral, propelled not by a willed or chosen meaning, but simply by the plausibility of each moment's yearning for the next. To the despair of Christians, this spiral is good enough for most men. As Pascal said, it casts an 'incomprehensible spell' on them, giving them a kind of 'supernatural torpor' in the face of death itself. They are like those condemned prisoners who in the very hour of their execution astonish their executioners by the avidity with which they wolf down their last meal.[22]

This indifference to mortality was the scandal of unredeemed human nature for Augustinians, and they regarded an unremitting sense of the shadow which death casts over earthly striving as a spiritual pre-condition of righteousness. This horror is the most necessary of Grace's gifts: it is the fear that creates the longing for a bliss beyond anything the body could ever know.

As a moment of truth, the hour of death stands in a double relation to need. It is our 'hour of need', the time when we are most dependent on the consolation of our fellow men and women; it is the time we make our ultimate claim upon them, test their loyalty and even discover their betrayal. 'Where were you in my hour of need?' is a reproach that is heard from beyond the grave.

If the secular vision of life as a spiral of needs makes the claim that human life can be lived without spiritual consolation, in Augustinian discourse death is the fact which disproves the claim. As secular people we may claim that ultimate questions about the ends of human life are unanswerable in principle and therefore no business of ours, but each one of us has our hour of need. However blind life on the spiral may be, there is one hour when it all stops. What then will we say? What then will we need?

If we stand back from these Christian mystics, painters and saints, and ask ourselves these questions about the needs of our dying moments – the needs of our spirit – it is remarkable how individual our answers are likely to be. We no longer share a vision of the good death. Most other cultures, including many primitive ones whom we have subjugated to our reason and our technology, enfold their members in an art of dying as in an art of living. But we have left these awesome tasks of culture to private choice. Some of us face our deaths with a rosary, some with a curse, some in company, some alone. Some die bravely, to give courage to the living, while others die with no other audience than their lonely selves. Some of us need a cosmology in which we can see the spark that is our life, and some of us go to our deaths needing nothing more than the gaze of another to console us in the hour of our departing.

If Augustine and Bosch, Pascal and Erasmus were to see us now, they would be dismayed, but not surprised. A world of beings utterly unaware of spiritual need is precisely the possibility which the doctrine of original sin set itself to explain. As Augustine, Pascal and Bosch so profoundly understood, moreover, the great enemy of religion is not science, nor the active profession of unbelief, but rather the silent and pervasive plausibility of earthly need as a metaphysics of ordinary life. In the desires and needs of the body, human life can find all its justification.

It is not the development of material need which sets the modern vocabulary of aspiration apart from anything which has gone before, but rather the transformation of our spiritual needs. It is our spirits, not our clothes and houses and cars, that set us so radically apart from our own past and from much of the rest of the world. Imagine what we must be like to the primitive peoples who receive our attentions as anthropologists. We come upon them armed with our mastery of nature, and yet they can disarm us with the simplest metaphysical inquiry: what happens when people die? where do they go? what are the duties of the living to the dead? Their cultures are as rich in answers to these questions as our culture is rich in answers to the technical and scientific problems which baffle them.

It has always been a truism of the Western bad conscience that we have purchased our mastery of nature at the price of our spirits.

The conservative and romantic critique of Western progress has always used the example of the savage – rich in cosmology, poor in goods – to argue for an inverse historical relationship between the development of material and spiritual needs. Certainly this view could draw upon the dark side of the Christian theology of need. While secular optimists have trusted in the permanence of spiritual need, Augustinian Christians have fixed their gaze on the nightmare of the happy slave: the being so absorbed by the material that all spiritual needs have perished.

Yet human needing is historical, and who can predict what forms the needs of the spirit may take? There is a loss of nerve in the premature announcements of the death of the spirit, the easy condemnations of materialist aspiration in capitalist society. Western societies have continued the search for spiritual consolation in the only manner consistent with the freedom of the seeking subject: by making every person the judge of his own spiritual satisfaction. We have all been left to choose what we need, and we have pushed the search for private meaning to the limits of what a public language can contain if it is to continue to be a means of communication. We have Augustine's first freedom, and because we have it, we cannot have his second. We can no longer offer each other the possibility of metaphysical belonging: a shared place, sustained by faith, in a divine universe. All our belonging now is social.

What would astonish a primitive tribesman about the state of our spirits is that we believe we can establish the meaningfulness of our private existence in the absence of any collective cosmology or teleology. The priest of this particular kind of pursuit is Freud. The needs of our spirit have been re-born in the intensive search for the logic of our childhood, our dreams, our desires. We share with other tribes the idea that certain forms of knowledge are necessary to our health, but we are the only tribe which believes that such necessary knowledge can be private knowledge – the science of the individual. We have created a new need, the need to live an examined life; we pursue its satisfaction in the full babble of conflicting opinions about what life is for, and we pursue it in a collectively held silence about the meaning of death. Instead of being astonished at the spiritual emptiness of the times, we should be amazed that individuals manage, in both the silence and the babble, to find sufficient meaning and purpose.

Without knowing it, we have been living this way for a very long time, at least since the European Enlightenment. It was then that philosophers began to try, by their own example and by their writing, to demonstrate that a secular market society could provide competitive individuals with sufficient reasons for co-operating, and for living. They tried to imagine the moral logic of a society without confessional unity or shared belief. In returning to their work, we can recover the shock of the world we have become used to. One of the first philosophers to cast his mind forward to the world we live in was David Hume. It is to his living, and to his dying, that we should now turn.

3 · METAPHYSICS AND THE MARKET

... in the last scene, between death and ourselves, there is no more pretending; we must talk plain French ...

MONTAIGNE

James Boswell records in his diary that 'on Sunday forenoon the 7 of July 1776, being too late for church', he decided to walk over to St Andrew's Square in Edinburgh to pay a visit to 'Mr. David Hume, who was returned from London and Bath, just a dying.'[1] Boswell, who had courted the great philosopher's friendship for a decade, found him alone in a reclining posture in the drawing-room. Hume was 'lean, ghastly, and quite of an earthy appearance, dressed in a suit of grey cloth with white metal buttons and a kind of scratch wig'. Despite his condition, Hume's habitual good nature did not desert him even now, and he exchanged pleasantries with his young friend until Boswell guided the conversation into the sombre terrain of immortality.

Hume was the most notorious enemy of revealed religion in Europe after Voltaire, and with a journalist's callous instinct for a story, Boswell hoped perhaps to coax the old man towards some publishable grave-side recantations. But Boswell's motives went deeper than that: he was disturbed by the old man's calm indifference to consolations which Boswell, no less than his mentor in London, Dr Johnson, could not live his erring life without. 'I had a strong curiosity', Boswell recalled, 'to be satisfied if he persisted in disbelieving a future state even when he had death before his eyes. I asked him if the thought of annihilation never gave him any uneasiness.' No more uneasiness, Hume replied, than the thought that he had not existed before his birth. He said he was very happy as he was – the sun was shining, and the chances were very much against his being so well in an afterlife. Boswell said tensely that he hoped they would meet in Heaven and that he would prove him wrong. If there were an afterlife, Hume mused, he supposed he could give as good an account of himself as any Christian.

83

Hume said all this, Boswell remembered when he set it down in his diary afterwards, 'with his usual grunting pleasantry, with that thick breath which fatness had rendered habitual to him, and that smile of simplicity which his good humour constantly produced'. They moved on to easier topics, of which Boswell chiefly remembered Hume's irritation with the shallowness and absurdity of Lord Monboddo's treatise on *The Origin of Language*, and his enthusiasm for his friend Adam Smith's *Wealth of Nations*, both published in that year. The conversation between them was as amusing as it always was with Hume, but when he went away and left the old man alone Boswell was seized 'with a degree of horror, mixed with a sort of wild, strange, hurrying recollection of my excellent mother's pious instructions, of Dr Johnson's noble lessons, and of my religious sentiments and affections during the course of my life'.

On 8 August, a month after Boswell's visit, it was Adam Smith's turn to pay a call on Hume. Finding him seemingly as spry as ever Smith ventured to express hopes of a recovery. Hume was cheerful and brisk. 'Your hopes are groundless. An habitual diarrhoea of more than a year's standing would be a very bad disease at any age: at my age it is a mortal one.' He was content with the span he had attained – sixty-five was a great age in those times – and in any event he had concluded that his illness was fatal and had said as much in his short autobiography, completed several months before. He had said then that he looked forward to 'a speedy dissolution': it was in fact to be protracted and painful.[2]

Smith then said that if it must be so, at least his old friend knew that he had managed to leave all his friends and relations in great prosperity. Hume had indeed taken special care that his relations were provided for, and he had submitted to the discomfort of lengthy farewell visits with them by sedan chair. The thought that all the mortal knots of his life had been tied seemed to please the old man greatly. He told Smith that he had been recently re-reading one of his favourite books, Lucian's *Dialogues of the Dead*, and had read over the excuses which the dying offered to the boatman, Charon, to spare them the final voyage across the river Styx.[3] But no excuse fitted him. He had no house to finish, no daughter to provide for, no enemy upon whom to visit revenge. For a time indeed he had been at a loss for a good reason to tarry on the river's edge. Then it had occurred to him that he might ask Charon for a little more time to prepare his works for a new edition. Hume was an inveterate reviser of his works, and, in his last years, had been retouching his most fundamental attack on Christian metaphysics, the *Dialogues Concerning Natural Religion*. But he reflected that Charon was hardly likely to allow time for an author's vanity. He told Smith, impishly, that he might just ask Charon for enough time to see mankind delivered from Christian superstition. But he already knew Charon's answer: 'That won't happen these two hundred years. Into the boat this instant, you lazy, loitering rogue.'[4]

Twenty-five years of friendship closed with this wry classical joke. Smith never saw Hume again. They wrote to each other once more, Hume pleading that Smith take charge of posthumous publication of the *Dialogues*, Smith wavering to the last between the obligations of friendship and his disinclination to be associated with a work of 'atheism'. At the very end, Hume must have known that Smith would not carry out his dying wishes.[5] And so it turned out. When the *Dialogues* did appear in 1779, Smith had nothing to do with their publication.

Hume died on 25 August 1776. Four days later, hung over and contrite after a night with the whores, Boswell stood soaking in the rain by the churchyard wall and watched as the procession of carriages came down from St Andrew's Square bearing the coffin to its rest.

The serenity of Hume's final hours became one of the talking points in the battle between the Enlightenment's party of humanity and the party of faith. Smith published an account of

the last days of his 'perfectly wise and virtuous friend' in early
1777, and the little pamphlet proved more controversial at the
time than his *Wealth of Nations*.[6] His account of Hume's light-
hearted banter at the edge of the grave profoundly shocked many
Christians. It drove one bishop to reply indignantly in a public
letter to Smith:

Are you sure, can you make us sure, that there really exists no such
thing as a God, and a future state of rewards and punishments? If so,
all is well. Let us then in our last hours read Lucian, and play at whist
and droll upon Charon and his boat; let us die as foolish and insensible,
as much like our brother philosophers, the calves of the field and the
asses of the desert, as we can, for the life of us. But if such things *be* –
as they most certainly are – is it right in you, Sir, to hold up to our view,
as 'perfectly wise and virtuous' the character and conduct of one who
seems to have been possessed with an incurable antipathy to all that is
called Religion?[7]

Others refused to take Hume's philosophical death seriously.
Johnson told Boswell that the atheist's serenity was only a pose,
'an appearance of ease' to confound believers. Edmund Burke
was more sardonic: atheists, he told Boswell, had their church
no less than believers. Hume's death and Smith's account were
'done for the credit of their Church', and well done too, though
it was a trifle exaggerated to make such a fuss about a man of
the ripe old age of sixty-five, who had been preparing a Socratic
death all along.[8]

We owe it to Hume's death to keep alive its capacity for
instruction. Yet this is not easy. To the extent that most of us die
now without religious consolation, we may fail to understand
Boswell's terror when he watched a man die in this new way. For
terror it genuinely was, and not just a voyeur's shiver of pleasure.
In the weeks after his interview with Hume, he skulked around
the philosopher's house, seeking entry once or twice, only to be
turned away by tearful servants. He went to the Advocates'
Library and 'from a kind of self-tormenting inclination' read

Hume's essays on miracles again, recoiling, so we can imagine, from the slice of the razor in the sentence: 'So that on the whole we may conclude that the Christian religion not only was at first attended with miracles, but that even at this day cannot be believed by any reasonable person without one.'[9]

Hume's eerie serenity haunted Boswell for months, indeed years, after that final interview. Many months after Hume's death, we come upon an entry in Boswell's diary describing a Sunday morning on which he lay in bed talking to his infant daughter Veronica. He asked the little girl what she would do if she were to die and go to Heaven and not him find there, but instead saw him shut out in the bleak wastes of purgatory beyond the walls of the heavenly city. When she said brightly that she would go up to God and ask him to let her father in, Boswell hugged her tightly with relief.[10]

We no longer speak to anyone, let alone our children, like this, and if Boswell's terror is still our own, the consolation of the child's reply is no longer available to most of us.

There are other embarrassments in the story. It is hard to imagine ourselves actually asking a philosopher such mortal questions as Boswell dared ask Hume. Yet poor old Boswell – brash, even contemptible voyeur of another man's dying – may have had it right after all. What we still want from any man of wisdom, after we have had all his mental ingenuity, is what Boswell wanted so brazenly from Hume: to know how we are to get through this life of ours 'with death in our eye'. We may not have the right to ask this of every philosopher, but Boswell had the right to ask it of Hume, because he had committed himself to an answer.

In a letter to Francis Hutcheson, the professor of moral philosophy at Glasgow, written in 1739 when he was just twenty-eight, Hume had asked ironically, 'For pray what is the end of Man? Is he created for Happiness? Or for Virtue? For this life or the next? For himself or his Maker?' Whatever answer reason tried to offer to such questions, he said, was bound to be 'pretty uncertain and unphilosophical'.[11] No philosopher was more merciless towards the human weakness for asking unanswerable questions. If today there is a mocking echo in the phrase 'the meaning of life', Hume figures prominently in the history of that irony. Such 'abstruse questions' he insisted in the first Enquiry, were 'utterly inaccessible to the understanding'.[12] Nothing in human experience offered the slightest evidence of an ultimate purpose for mankind's confused and contradictory strivings.

This conclusion was more than a dry inference from epistemology. As Hume revealed in the anguished conclusion to the first book of his *Treatise of Human Nature*, written during his retreat in Anjou when he was just twenty-five, the discovery that reason was powerless to answer the ultimate questions of life had been paid for in the hard coinage of personal experience. The equanimity of his final hours was beaten out on the lonely forge of his twenties. He had felt then, as he struggled with the ideas of causation, free will and necessity, that his solitary studies had twisted him into 'some strange uncouth monster, who not being able to mingle and unite in society, has been expell'd all human commerce'.[13] The 'perplexity, the gradual bafflement of reason itself', the sense of being 'inviron'd with the deepest darkness', which Hume lived through in those years gave him, he realized ironically, experience in common with religious mystics. Like them, he had known 'the coldness and desertion of spirits' which attends waiting for the hidden God.[14] Like Pascal and the Jansenists of Port Royal, like the earnest young Jesuits he conversed with in the cloisters of La Flèche while he was composing the *Treatise*, Hume had followed the mind's insatiability for proofs into the bare room of doubt, and like them he had had to learn the lessons of renunciation – not the trust of faith, but trust in the certainties of secular passion. He discovered that when reason was incapable of dispelling the clouds of philosophical melancholy, Nature herself came to the rescue with the merciful diversions of sense and society.

I dine, I play a game of backgammon, I converse and am merry with my friends; and when after three or four hours' amusement, I wou'd return to these speculations, they appear so cold and strain'd, and ridiculous, that I cannot find in my heart to enter into them any further.[15]

Ever after, it remained a task of his philosophy to explain why the existential certainty that philosophy laboured to ground in rational proof was so artlessly and effortlessly delivered by the everyday happiness of life.

We are not likely to be impressed by Hume's discovery that metaphysical darkness could be dissipated by 'action and employment and the occupations of common life'.[16] Yet it is worth considering the positions arrayed against such an apparently obvious idea. Consider these ancient priorities: 'Seek ye *first* the kingdom of God.' 'Man does not live by bread alone.' These priorities were the stuff of the *Whole Duty of Man*, the devotional text of Hume's childhood, and of such other works of Presbyterian piety as we can suppose a Scottish laird's earnest but already sceptical son to have imbibed at the family property of Ninewells.[17] His vindication of the existentially soothing properties of the flesh also had arrayed against it the beloved Stoic authors of his adolescence, who counselled a life of willed indifference to the things of this world, the better to prepare oneself for the hour of death. We can judge by Hume's own death how much he treasured the Stoic ideal of self-command, which makes his rejection of their view of the self-deceptions of passion the more original.

Certainly the seventeenth-century Augustinians, whom Hume read carefully, would not have had much good to say for the metaphysically soothing properties of backgammon. Weren't such games precisely the 'diversions' which Pascal had said kept ordinary men from facing up to their spiritual desolation? Yet in other ways Hume was close to the austere Jansenists of Port Royal.[18] Their rejection of the rational God of reasoners, their insistence that God is hidden, ineffable, known through His mysterious Grace, never through human cogitation, recall his own satires on the presumptions of human reason in theological matters.

The person in Hume's formation who built this peculiar bridge between faith and scepticism was Pierre Bayle, the French Protestant in exile in Amsterdam after the Edict of Nantes. His *Dictionary* and its hilarious and learned footnotes became a mine for eighteenth-century anti-religious polemic, but he himself seems to have remained a believer. A remark in his *Dictionary* entry on Spinoza seems to define the resting place of his private faith:

There are . . . people whose religion is in the heart, and not in the mind. The moment they seek it by human reasoning, they lose sight of it; it eludes the subtleties and sophistries of their processes of argument; when they try to weigh up the pros and cons, they become confused; but as soon as they stop arguing, and simply listen to the evidence of their feelings, the instinctive promptings of their conscience, the legacy of their upbringing, and so on, they are convinced by a religion and live their lives by it, so far as human infirmity allows.[19]

It is in Bayle's work that we see the lines of transmission from 'fideism', the submission of faith, to 'scepticism', doubt in the capacity of reason to know God or divine his rules for human conduct. The Humian attack on religion simply drove home the critique of the insufficiency of human reason already made by the seventeenth-century believers like Bayle.

Another of Hume's favourite seventeenth-century writers, Father Malebranche, once wrote that the chief source of human sin was the fact that our 'passions all justify themselves'. Hume insisted that without these justifications, human life would be at a standstill. If motive had to be grounded in rational argument, life would be the questioning nightmare that it had been for

Hume in his twenties.[20] Happily it did not. 'Nature is always too strong for principle.' Man's 'natural necessities' – what we would call his needs – impel him forward on the path to their satisfaction even when reason questions the ultimate worth of the chase.

To Hume, the impetuous pressure of our needs seemed to cast a clear light in the dark debate about God's intentions for man. Pleasure and satisfaction prove their worth as motives in the unmistakable coinage of sensation. No other ends of human life are immune from rational doubt. In hunger appeased, thirst slaked, resentment gratified, pity displayed and sexual desire sated, sensation consecrates the chase, validates all toil.

Without the certainties of pleasure, the very survival of the species would be stalled by rational doubt. In their beds, humans give themselves to the spiral of desire, without a thought to the welfare of the species, the future of their children, indeed to anything at all.[21] On the fact that desire does not halt before rational calculation the future of life on the planet depends. And likewise human progress. If human striving were to resign itself to death, as reason says we must, such victories as we do achieve over death – law and government, science and art – would never be attempted. It is the 'happy artifice of nature' – the persuasiveness of our needs and desires – that deceives us into a conviction that our Promethean labours are not in vain.[22] No philosophical opinion, however cogent or beloved, has the same power to validate life for the living as the ache of desire and the plenitude of satisfaction.[23]

Smith's *Theory of Moral Sentiments*, published in 1759 when he was in his early thirties and just beginning his life-long friendship with Hume, plays variations on these essentially Humian themes. In theory, the Stoics might be right: 'those great objects of human desire' – power and riches – are hardly worth the candle. Neither can purchase immunity from the central trials of human life – 'anxiety, fear, sorrow, diseases, danger and death'.[24] But it is just as well, Smith goes on, that 'nature imposes on us in this manner'. The blind certainties of need are the invisible hand driving human beings towards achievements before which reason would otherwise falter.

When Hume and Smith made basic need rather than rational choice the motor of progress,[25] they did so with a strong sense of the provocation their doctrines offered to the Stoic and Christian depreciation of material need. As Smith told his students:

All the arts, the sciences, law and government, wisdom and even virtue itself tend all to this one thing, the providing meat, drink, rayment and lodging for men, which are commonly reckoned the meanest of employments and fit for the pursuit of none but the meanest and lowest of the people.[26]

Or, as Hume said, social life was held together not by 'passion for public good' but by 'a spirit of avarice and industry, art and luxury'.[27]

Their account of 'hunger, thirst and the passion for sex'[28] as the motor of historical progress may have shocked religious sensibilities, but their theory of need was an answer to an essentially religious question: how human beings manage to get through their lives with 'death in their eye'; how most human beings, as Boswell confessed to a friend, may not be able to say *how* they get through their life, but nonetheless 'get through it very well'.[29]

This emphasis on the saving certainties of passion helps to explain why, if Hume was a metaphysical sceptic, he was not a sceptic in morals. Human beings might be in darkness about the ultimate ends of life, but they need not be in darkness as to their moral duties here and now. As he wrote, all duties are divided into two categories, those 'impelled by a natural instinct or immediate propensity', such as love of children, gratitude to benefactors, pity to the unfortunate, and those performed 'from a sense of obligation when we consider the necessities of human society'.

The duties of this second sort are those of justice – regard to the property of others, observance of promises and contracts, and so on.[30] All human morality, therefore, derives from our natural needs or our social ones, our beliefs about the necessities of human society.[31] Awareness of our common necessities makes us capable of grasping the intelligibility of each other's conduct and thus of trusting each other.[32] Consciousness of necessity guides human conduct in a universe whose ultimate purpose is wrapped in darkness.[33] Since people share the same needs, they can agree on the minimum preconditions of moral behaviour, in particular their obligation to relieve the needs of others in distress. The common belief in the utility of these arrangements is then undergirded by the natural human attributes of pity and sympathy reinforced by habit and custom.[34]

A secular ethics, grounded solely in the facts of human need and human belief, is as solid a basis for human conduct as one grounded in the idea that we owe an account of the stewardship of our lives to our Master.[35] Hume maintained that while individuals might disagree interminably about the proper objects of human desire, they could make minimal binding agreements about what they all needed, in institutions of justice and property, and in rules of moral conduct. On this human capacity to agree on the identity of human need, virtue, order and progress depend.

Yet there is an obvious difficulty: in a capitalist society, or as Hume would have said a 'commercial society', economic growth constantly expands the frontier of necessity. The luxuries of the few gradually become the necessities of all. If moral virtue depends on common agreement about necessity, how is moral virtue possible in a society which is constantly pushing back the limits of need?[36]

In all the moral traditions that confronted the coming of capitalist modernity, the man of virtue was the man of few needs: in the Stoic discourse, the man of self-command; in the religious discourses of Calvinism and Jansenism, the saint; in Renaissance civic humanism, the citizen; in the reveries of Scottish Lowland gentry like James Boswell, the austere, Highland chieftain.[37] From the moment that European commerce began to press its imperium into the forest, jungle and savannah of the Americas, this judging figure took on the guise of the savage. Chained and beaten though he was in the plantations of his masters, he roamed free in their conscience, judging both their cruelty and the triviality of those desires – for cocoa, molasses, cotton and fur – of which imperialism was itself the slave.

The savage's virtue, as Diderot, Raynal and Rousseau argued, was premised on economic autarky, on his self-reliance as hunter-gatherer in the lost paradise before mine and thine. He had only such needs as his fleetness, cunning and the contingent bounty of his world made possible. His virtue was insulated from temptation, because his self-regard was indifferent to the stranger's gaze.[38]

In all these forms – Stoic hero, saint, citizen and savage – the man of few needs served to pass judgement on the modern man of vanity. Economic man assembles his sense of self not from autonomous self-regard but from the mirror gaze of other men.[39] His desires are insatiable because they are relative to other men's desiring; his lust for riches, as Hume admitted, is 'insatiable, perpetual, universal' and if unchecked by the rules of justice, 'directly destructive of society'.[40] His virtue, Rousseau bitterly added, is a deceiving mask.[41]

Hume and Smith's reply to this indictment of the false consciousness of economic man was to insist on his intransigent individualism.[42] It was not merely that he is the best judge of his needs, but that he only values them if they are authentically his own. He can know them as his own by standing outside himself, outside the social game of mirrors, and seeing himself as an impartial spectator might. Rousseau, Diderot and other exponents of capitalist man's inveterate capacity for insatiable deception supposed that he surrenders his moral autonomy to the mirror game of social competition. Hume and Smith continued to suppose a sovereign self, capable of winnowing the truth of desire from mediation. This is the cunning use to which nature puts our ostensibly asocial individualism: society is saved from false consciousness by the self's intransigent desire to know its desire as its own. This may be the only possible rebuttal to doctrines of false-consciousness in this or any time, but it is one that places a heavy wager of faith on capitalist economic man's powers of will.

In the manner of his own dying, Hume certainly vindicated the human capacity for self-command, but in his own philosophy, he tended to rate the capacities of ordinary mortals much lower: such virtue as they possess depends on the schooling of their passions by habit, custom and opinion; such wills as they have, he said, are the playthings of their emotions, not the servants of their reason.[43] His relatively sunny assessment of capitalist man's capacities for virtue 'in the great scramble' of commercial society depends, in the last instance, on a faith in the autonomous self and its capacities for self-command, which in his own philosophy barely seems to survive the caustic of his own scepticism.

Moreover, his argument that ordinary living and dying does not require a metaphysics presumes a degree of moral calm in secular man which his own social psychology of religious experience tends to contradict. For as he himself realized, the idea that men have no natural need of metaphysical consolation assumes that they find nothing problematic about human nature. Yet both his *Natural History of Religion* and *Dialogues Concerning Natural Religion* argue that the need for religious consolation arises in human history precisely because we are unreconciled to what we are, and seek through religion to explain the pain of our own natures.

Those who see the hand of Providence in the economy of human nature would have to explain, he wrote, why the human species 'is of all others the most necessitous and the most deficient in bodily advantages; without Cloaths, without Arms, without

Food and Lodging, without any Convenience of Life, except what they owe to their own skill and industry'.[44]

In other species, need is in equilibrium with habitat. The lion's strength, the lamb's meekness, are finely adjusted to their respective appetites and habitat, while man's reach fatally exceeds his grasp. God would have been able to justify his ways to men if he had only given them a 'greater propensity to industry and labour; a more vigorous Spring and Activity of mind; a more constant Bent to Business and Application'. Inscrutably, the human frame was so contrived that 'nothing but the most violent necessity can oblige' man to labour. Man's needs and scarcities are both impossible to reconcile with Providential design in human nature. Philo, the sceptic in Hume's *Dialogues*, remarks in mockery of religious anthropomorphism that an 'indulgent Parent' ought to have provided somewhat more generously for his sons and daughters.[45]

Some Providential optimists professed to see the indulgent parent at work, if not in man's needs, then in his social achievements.[46] It is true, Hume said, that human beings more than any other species have it in their power to compensate for their natural weakness through the division of labour. Yet these are purely human achievements, he insists, not the work of Providential good intentions. They are not coded, as it were, in the logic of human needing itself. While some needs – notably the 'natural appetite betwixt the sexes' – are centripetal and pull human beings together, others – notably the 'insatiable and perpetual' avidity for goods and possessions – pull them apart. It is only by painful historical experience that man learns to harness insatiability for goods within the shafts of justice. When Hume called justice an 'artificial' virtue, he meant that it is a human achievement, not a Providential pre-adaptation of human nature to the demands of social life.[47]

To think that God adapted our natures to the demands of social existence is to wish away the conflict between duty and desire, the commonest torment of moral life. It is not because the design of human pain is evident, but precisely because it is inscrutable, that men are moved by their suffering to search the skies for 'the obscure traces of divinity'.[48] The religious impulse is not an autonomous need in itself, like hunger or thirst, but a derivative of them. Religious devotion, Hume wrote, 'springs not from an original instinct or primary impression of nature, such as gives rise to self-love, affection between the sexes, love of progeny, gratitude, resentment'.[49] If we could imagine the human animal without physical necessities and without scarcity, he would be utterly without religious impulse. Religion represents man's reflection on his needs, his attempt to find a cosmology adequate to explain the pain intrinsic to their satisfaction in a world of scarcity.

The God which men invented as the author of their suffering – the loving Father whose punishments turn out for the best in the fullness of time – was a mournful proof for Hume of how little truth men can bear about their situation. Were they to invent a God faithful to their actual experience of the world, a very different image would result. In a passage he added to the *Dialogues* when he was already dying, Hume said there was only one vision of God actually consistent with the facts of the human situation. If such a creature exists, he wrote – not now with that genial serenity Boswell was to encounter but with the passionate intensity of the dying – it must be some kind of bound and blind creature, impregnated by the elemental force of life and ceaselessly giving birth in groans and travail to the animal and human creation, 'her maim'd and abortive children'.[50]

Perhaps now we are in a better position to understand something of Boswell's disquiet at that last interview. The core of the Humian claim in morals is that we need not know anything certain about the ultimate ends of life in order to discharge our obligations. Indeed, we do not need to know why we do anything: our needs themselves pick us up and carry our reason and will along. Yet in the darker places of his religious thought, one encounters a very different proposition indeed: human needing, unlike animal needing, is neither functional, adaptive nor resigned. Men do not merely *have* their needs: they seek to make them bearable by compassing them in meaning, in the language of Providence, in the mythology of original sin.

Hume's hidden kinship with the Augustinians is evident here: both locate the dynamic of spiritual need in the human understanding that our nature is unendurable and its economy inscrutable. Of course, Hume makes spiritual need a purely human phenomenon, while to the Augustinians, this yearning is kindled by Grace.[51] Hume indeed is the starting-point of the modern study of religion as a purely human institution.[52] Yet if the divide between the two discourses is unbridgeable at this point, they touch at another unexpected place: in their realization that human beings are capable of realizing their alienation from the natural world and from themselves. What we need, therefore, is very much more than what we are.

As much as we need food, clothes and shelter, we need to know *why*, but no human language is adequate to the question. Needing itself cannot answer the problem of human pain. Its economy is inscrutable and in its presence, there cannot be understanding; there can only be will, good humour, a joke with Charon at the water's edge.

Perhaps it is no wonder that if this is what Hume believed, Boswell should have dreamed, six years after the philosopher's death, that he had found a secret diary in which the old man confessed to himself that he had been a true and devout believer all along. It was, Boswell said, 'a very agreeable dream'.[53] It was also evidence for the Humian contention that what a man does not want to believe, he can find a way to deny.

There are other denials, more desperate than pious dreams. Thucydides once remarked how in cities visited by the plague, men and women would be seized with insatiable lust and couple openly with each other in the doorways and in the streets. Boccaccio likewise reported that in Italian city states under siege, the doomed citizens would take frenzied pleasure with each other among the ruins.[54] Where life is darkened by death, the philosopher's self-command demands too much of the common run of men. Hume was fond of both these examples of his own argument.

Months after Hume's death, Boswell took a woman of the streets up to some waste ground behind St Andrew's Square and coupled with her in the squalid darkness of a mason's shed. He did this thing often enough, but in this case, there was something a little different. Can it have been accidental that he should have noted in his diary that it all took place 'just a stone's throw from David Hume's house'?[55] If this too was a refusal, then it was one which the old philosopher would have understood better than most.

Yet it was a refusal which in its infantile provocation of the dead father-figure showed how poorly need obeys that spectatorial restraint which Hume trusted to civilize our passions. It is one thing to imagine a morality sheared away from divine sanction if you are, like Hume, the stoic master of your needs; but quite another if you are, like Boswell, their reckless and compulsive slave. It is one thing to imagine a world without a forgiving Father if you are, like Hume, at peace with yourself; quite another if, like Boswell, you can barely stand yourself at all. A purely secular morality is an ethics without ultimate forgiveness. Boswell in his terror saw that clearly enough.

Hume saw it too and simply waved away the blindfolds of Christian consolation. There is a certain grandeur in this mocking refusal to surrender to the common needs of men in the hour of their death. Secular culture has rarely kept this grandeur since. Secularism today simply implies a generalized silence in culture about the whole category of man's spiritual needs. In Hume's Socratic death, it meant a principled refusal of these needs.

Hume was too sceptical to look forward to the historical wasting away of these needs, but there soon came others in his century – Condorcet, for example – who took the historicization of need to its logical conclusion.[56] If credulity is paired with scarcity, poverty and ignorance, might there not be a society that by abolishing scarcity could abolish the need for spiritual self-deception? Feed the body and the spirit will cease to hunger. Give all men liberty, equality and fraternity and they will stop surrendering their will and intelligence to the dominion of priests.

The Communist utopia stands as the heir and end of this Enlightenment dream of secular redemption, the completion in reality of that critique of religion which German ideology had only undertaken in thought. If men could be freed from the grip of scarcity, if the basic antagonism between human creatures – the class struggle – could be abolished, the human need for metaphysical consolation would vanish as a fading superstition of the past.[57]

Yet it is exactly here that the grandeur of Marx's Promethean conception of man as the master of his fate reveals its vanity. We are natural creatures as well as social ones, and our fate is not always in our hands. There is much that we can suffer which justice, equality and fraternity can redeem, but there is much else we cannot do anything about: illness, aging, separation and death.[58] True enough, some societies help individuals to bear these burdens with greater dignity than others. It is even possible that modern societies – capitalist or socialist, it doesn't matter – are impoverished in those rituals of mourning and grieving which help peasant societies to shift the unbearable pain of existence from one back to many. Yet the sharing of suffering can only distribute the burden. When the villagers and relatives have left the grave and the coffin has been lowered into the earth, the widow is still alone: she will be alone under any social dispensation we can imagine. Death is paired with loneliness even in societies rich in rituals for its sharing.

Marx is largely silent about the natural and unalterable elements of our destiny, and it was upon this silence that his utopia was built. It is possible to think of men's spiritual needs as the alienated form of their longing for justice and fraternity only so long as one chooses to be blind to the facts of our situation which no amount of social engineering can hope to change.

We have needs of the spirit because we are the only species whose fate is not simply a mute fact of our existence but a problem whose meaning we attempt to understand. Yet our answers change, and so do the languages of understanding in which we express these needs. The fact that our fate is unalterable does not make our needs immutable. We may yet encounter death and suffering in ways that are as unimaginable to us now as Hume's death was unimaginable to Boswell.

The death that shocked Boswell is ours now, and yet we still do not understand it. We are still coming to terms with what it means to die outside the fold of religious consolation.

In this long spiritual interregnum, our need for meaning is met – if it is met at all – by grief itself. The meaning of death lies only in what we feel about it. Hume's death – secular death – makes a massive gamble on the unalterable structure of human sentiment, on the naturalness of human feeling. If we cannot put our trust in Heaven or Charon the boatman, we can put our trust in grief, in the natural redemption of tears.

But what is to happen to those who cannot grieve, who cannot feel? We know from the secret history of human needing that Freud wrote for us how many people there are who have to live their lives without the consolation of natural emotion. They came to the consulting room at 19 Berggasse ill because they could not mourn, numbed by their own numbness, emptied by their emptiness.[59] They needed the reconciliation of grief, but unavowable pleasure at the death of those they loved would not allow them to find it.

Modern societies increasingly put their trust in the sciences of the self to unblock the channels between need and consciousness. They assist the lonely self to know what it feels and to feel what it knows. In doing so, these therapies are the expression of a metaphysics of feeling. If we could only know what we feel, we would know what it means. If we could know what we feel, we could bear it.

No other metaphysics may be possible, yet it is a fragile crutch. For at least a century Western literature has been exploring the moral universe of people who do not happen to feel the emotions their culture tells them they should feel: Madame Bovary bending over the cot of her own child and whispering to herself, 'God, how ugly that child is . . .', Meursault finding nothing but silence inside himself when asked to tell the court why he pulled the trigger on the young Algerian on the beach.[60] Our literature and our lives have taken us into realms of inner emptiness undreamed of in Hume's frame of reference.

Boswell understood better than most the loneliness of the modern self in its hour of need. As the first modern biographer – the first to include a great man's jests and table manners, his gait, his sleeping habits, his curses and his most private terrors in a narrative of selfhood – Boswell had thought deeply about what gives unity to a life. In his own diary, in that alternatively complacent, alternatively tortured account of the wayward path of his sexuality and ambition, the Socratic injunction to self-knowledge was pursued through the most ironic self-deception. For Hume the identity of the self, the core at the heart of that bundle of sensations, was merely an interesting technical problem in philosophy.[61] For Boswell the question went to the heart of the existential drama of his life. Over and over he asked himself where the centre of a man was, the core of commitment which desire could not move, the point of steadfastness from which his needs could at last be known. His demeaning and even pitiful courtship of fathers – Hume and Johnson – testifies to his failure to find that stable self. His need for forgiveness of every sort may strike us as extreme, yet it is closer to our own distrust in ourselves than Hume's serene composure. For Hume, spiritual need of Boswell's sort was a kind of pride, a yearning for certainties beyond the reach of human capacity. In this sense, these needs were a form of alienation. He said we could face the worst if we simply renounced our yearning for certainty. But who among us is capable of that renunciation?

4 · THE MARKET AND THE REPUBLIC

In civilized society [a man] stands at all times in need of the co-operation and assistance of great multitudes, while his whole life is scarce sufficient to gain the friendship of a few friends.

SMITH

Keeping citizens apart has become the first maxim of modern politics.

ROUSSEAU

Political utopias are a form of nostalgia for an imagined past projected on to the future as a wish. Whenever I try to imagine a future other than the one towards which we seem to be hurtling, I find myself dreaming a dream of the past. It is the vision of the classical *polis* – the city-state of ancient Greece and renaissance Italy – which beckons me backwards, as it were, into the future. No matter that Greek democracy was built upon the institution of slavery; no matter that the Italian city-states were feuding and unequal oligarchies. Utopias never have to make their excuses to history; like all dreams they have a timeless immunity to disappointment in real life. The *polis* would continue to beckon us forward out of the past even if no actual *polis* had ever existed.

Its human dimensions beckon us still: small enough so that each person would know his neighbour and could play his part in the governance of the city, large enough so that the city could feed itself and defend itself; a place of intimate bonding in which the private sphere of the home and family and the public sphere of civic democracy would be but one easy step apart; a community of equals in which each would have enough and no one would want more than enough; a co-operative venture in which work would be a form of collaboration among equals. Small, co-operative, egalitarian, self-governing and autarkic: these are the conditions of belonging that the dream of the *polis* has bequeathed to us.

It was in the late eighteenth century that the classical republican ideal of a polity that was master of itself first confronted the reality of a world capitalist economy. As David Hume lay dying in the house overlooking St Andrew's Square in those lingering summer months of 1776, the first battles of the American War of Independence were being fought in the fields and lanes of

Massachusetts thousands of miles away. As heirs of the classical republican ideal, the Americans were steeped in the precept that economic and political independence were necessary to each other. In their struggle against the Navigation Acts, they were attempting much more than protecting the sectional interests of their seaboard merchants: they were trying to realize the classical republican ideal in a global imperial market.

By the late eighteenth century too, European penetration of the primitive world was transforming the needs of non-Europeans, drawing them inexorably into dependence on Western goods. The people who came to trade furs and fish in return for beads and guns and alcohol were – to many Europeans – like the primitive Adam, exchanging the plenitude and innocence of Eden for the terrible knowledge of good and evil and eternal subjection to the craving for more.[1] On to the savage, European men projected their own doubts and disillusions about progress. When Locke had said, 'In the beginning, all was America', he meant that it was the American tribes who offered that image of autarkic virtue and happiness which Europeans themselves had enjoyed before they surrendered to the spiral of need.[2] In this new imperial context, in which Europeans could read the 'civilizing' of primitive man as the history of their own fall, the ancient republican ideal came to stand as the last best hope of finding a polity which, in subjecting men to a collective regime of autarkic self-restraint, would free them from enslavement to the spiral of material progress.

There is one particular intellectual encounter of the 1750s in which the republican ideal and the emerging world of the invisible hand face each other in stark antithesis. In March 1756, a thirty-three-year-old professor at the University of Glasgow, unknown to the world but acknowledged by his friends as an 'ingenious and learned gentleman', wrote anonymously to Alexander Wedderburn's new periodical, *The Edinburgh Review*, to warn that it risked extinction unless it extended the coverage of its reviews beyond the often 'absurd' local performances of Scottish writers to include the dramatic new philosophy of the Continent.[3] After mentioning Diderot and d'Alembert's *Encyclopédie*, whose first volumes had just appeared, the anonymous correspondent devoted the rest of his letter to a review of 'the late Discourse upon the origin and foundation of the inequality amongst mankind by Mr. Rousseau of Geneva'.

This is one of history's resonant little encounters – between Adam Smith, for this was the reviewer's name, and the already notorious Jean-Jacques – in the pages of a short-lived review published on the northernmost border of the European republic of letters. With hindsight, we can understand it as the first (and only) intellectual meeting between early capitalist society's most perceptive critic and its most penetrating theorist, then unknown but already leading students in his lectures along the chain of reasoning which was to conclude exactly twenty years later in the *Wealth of Nations*.

On the face of it, there was hardly a meeting of minds between Rousseau and Smith. When Rousseau said that 'ancient treatises of politics continually made mention of morals and virtue; ours speak of nothing but commerce and money', he was referring to certain French political economists, but he might just as well have been thinking of Smith.[4]

Yet we would be mistaken if we thought that Rousseau used only the language of morals and virtue, and Smith only that of commerce and money. Both writers insisted that the drama of human progress must be understood in its historical, moral and economic dimension: theirs was a vision that social science has since dispersed into the trackless capillaries of 'development studies' on the one hand and moralizing critiques of progress on the other.

Since both Smith and Rousseau were steeped in the natural jurisprudence tradition – in the writing of Grotius, Pufendorf and Locke – they both shared the same vision of history as a tumultuous passage of men from savage simplicity 'before mine and thine' to the modern world of private property and unequal social classes. The motor of this history was the interaction between the division of labour, the creation of surplus, the emergence of new needs, the foundation of private property and the unequal distribution of surplus among classes.

For Smith this blind upward spiral of needs delivers men from natural scarcity, and on this ground alone enlarges human freedom. For Rousseau, the spiral of needs is a tragedy of alienation. Rousseau insisted that man was once in Paradise, in a state of nature outside history, safe in the eternal present of primal satisfaction. There was no scarcity in this state of nature, and there could not be; as long as each man could appropriate nature as he pleased, nature provided enough room for all.[5] As long as men, Rousseau wrote, 'undertook only what a single person could accomplish, and confined themselves to such arts as did not require the joint labour of several hands, they lived free, honest and happy lives'. In other words, in a society in which there is no surplus, there is no scarcity; without surplus, need remains the limit of desire, and no one desires more than others. Anthropologists now tell us this is the equilibrium position of many hunting and gathering societies: the history of their needs is an eternal present.[6]

Rousseau saw no intrinsic reason why man in the state of nature should co-operate with others, as long as he could satisfy his needs himself. Smith, by contrast, argued that human beings are the only species for whom social co-operation in production and exchange is entirely natural:

Nobody ever saw a dog make a fair and deliberate exchange of one bone for another with another dog. Nobody ever saw one animal by its gestures and natural cries signify to another, this is mine, that yours.[7]

Our natural propensity to exchange, he argued, is a 'necessary consequence of the faculties of reason and speech'.

With exchange came specialization and the division of labour.[8] As tasks became specialized, the species began to realize its unique ability: to generate a surplus, to expand the scarcity constraints of nature and thus to release its own desire from the bounds of need.

Yet with surplus came property: the progressive individuation of the means of subsistence. By the time mankind had passed from the stage of hunters and gatherers to the period of settled agriculture, the human race was already divided between those who had property and those who were obliged to sell their labour.[9] However differently they understood the roots of human sociability, Smith and Rousseau were entirely at one in seeing the history of the division of labour as a history of human economic inequality. In a passage that Smith quoted in the *Edinburgh Review*, Rousseau made the connection between the division of labour and inequality explicit:

But from the instant in which one man had occasion for the assistance of another, from the moment that he perceived that it could be advantageous to a single person to have provisions for two, equality disappeared, property was introduced, labour became necessary, and the vast forests of nature were changed into agreeable plains, which must be watered with the sweat of mankind, and in which the world beheld slavery and wretchedness begin to grow up and blossom with the harvest.[10]

The challenge of this passage is taken up directly in the *Theory of Moral Sentiments*, which Smith was already giving as lectures to his students at the time of his review of Rousseau. He accepted that the emerging desire of the propertied to have more possessions than they need was a deception: happiness has nothing to do with possessions. But it was 'well that nature imposes on us in this manner. It is this deception which rouses and keeps in continual motion the industry of mankind.' In a passage whose choice of words is so close to those of Rousseau just quoted that it cannot be mere coincidence, Smith went on:

It is this which first prompted them to cultivate the ground, to build houses, to found cities and commonwealths, and to invent and improve all the sciences and arts, which ennoble and embellish human life; which have entirely changed the whole face of the globe, have turned the rude forests of nature into agreeable and fertile plains, and made the trackless and barren ocean a new fund of subsistence, and the great high road of communication to the different nations of the earth.[11]

Yet how is this panegyric to the human desire to accumulate wealth reconciled with the facts of inequality? How does the cunning of Nature turn men's potentially vicious desire to have more than they need into a means of providing for those who have not enough? Smith went on:

The rich only select from the heap what is most precious and agreeable. They consume little more than the poor, and in spite of their natural selfishness and rapacity, though they mean only their own conveniency, though the sole end which they propose from the labours of all the thousands whom they employ, be the gratification of their own vain and insatiable desires, they divide with the poor the produce of all their improvements. They are led by an invisible hand to make nearly the same distribution of the necessities of life, which would have been made, had the earth been divided into equal portions among all its inhabitants, and thus without intending it, without knowing it, advance the interest of society, and afford means to the multiplication of the species.[12]

The 'invisible hand' thus makes its appearance for the first time in Smith's work at a crucial moment: at the point where he shows how human progress can reconcile social inequality with adequate provision for the poorest. This argument continued to be the crux of Smith's defence of modernity in the *Wealth of Nations*. On the very first page of that book, in its 'Introduction and Plan', he remarked that in the 'savage nations of hunters and fishers, every individual who is able to work, is more or less employed in useful labour', while in 'civilized and thriving nations, a great number of people do not labour at all'; yet the former are frequently 'so miserably poor, that, from mere want, they are frequently reduced ... to the necessity sometimes of directly destroying their infants, their old people and those afflicted with lingering diseases, to perish with hunger'. In a civilized society, on the other hand, the 'produce of the whole labour of society is so great' that the labouring poor are able to support the huge burden of non-productive labourers and still enjoy 'a greater share of the necessaries and conveniences of life than it is possible for any savage to acquire'.[13]

Why inequality in modern commercial society should be compatible with the minimum degree of distributive justice to the poor, and why in more equal but backward societies, the poor starved, was the essential question which the *Wealth of Nations* set out to explain. To judge from Smith's *Early Drafts*, he had been pondering this question in the 1750s at exactly the moment he came across Rousseau's most passionate defence of the opposite proposition: that in commercial society 'the privileged few ... gorge themselves with superfluities, while the starving multitude are in want of the bare necessities of life'.[14]

Smith's division of labour argument explained how the productive labour of the poor in commercial society had been so increased that they could support both themselves and the mass of unproductive labourers (servants, professionals, artists, standing armies and the state). Rising productivity per man hour prevented the distributional conflict between rich and poor from becoming a zero-sum game: growth did not give the labourer a rising *relative* share of national income, but his *absolute* share in distribution did increase, so that, however simple his standard of comfort might be in comparison to the rich in his own society, it exceeded the standard of 'many an African king, the absolute master of the lives and liberties of ten thousand naked savages'.[15]

To this day, Smith's argument has provided modern capitalism with its most basic defence: only a system of private property offers the incentives necessary for technical innovation and economic progress. While a regime of private property is inevitably unequal, the growth that private property makes possible enables even the poorest to live decently. Capitalism vanquishes scarcity and, as such, is the only system of production with the capacity to extend to all the preconditions of human liberty.

Yet what Rousseau so clearly saw was that the very processes which freed men from their enslavement to natural scarcity in turn enslaved them to social scarcity. The very private-property regime that makes mastery of nature possible creates social inequalities which set off the rat race of competitive emulation. The history of progress is therefore the story of man exchanging natural alienation for social alienation, a battle with his fellows in place of a battle with the natural world.

Rousseau was not, as one might have expected, opposed to a society of abundance, but he insisted that such a society can never be virtuous, and its members reconciled to themselves and to each other, unless abundance is equalized.[16] If the unchecked tendency of the invisible hand in history is to reward the propertied, the first task of modern government is to 'prevent extreme inequality of fortune'. Politics must redress the natural injustice of history.

Rousseau's redistributive politics were always cautious and prudent. He left the right to bequeath property untouched: nothing, he said, 'is more fatal to morality and to the Republic than the continual shifting of rank and fortune among the citizens'.[17] Voltaire had thus misread Rousseau when he scribbled indignantly in the margins of his copy of of the *Second Discourse*, 'What! He who has planted, sown, fenced in, has no right to the fruit of his labour! What!'[18] As Rousseau made clear, justice requires absolute equality in the law's application: seizure of some people's property for the sake of other people violates this principle. 'The Sovereign has no right to touch the property of one or several individuals', just as the general will can legislate justly only if its laws apply to every single person who comprises it.[19] This leaves only one possibility: 'it may legitimately take possession of the property of all'. But even the redistribution of such property would have to observe strict equality among each of the individuals composing the general will. Rousseau left the option of communism unexplored.

The only just redistributive measure, Rousseau reasoned, would be a capitation tax on wealth and income, 'exactly proportioned to the circumstances of individuals'[20] as well as a tax on luxury goods. Taxes raise the price of luxuries for the rich but do not violate their liberty to waste their surplus on the 'frivolous and all too lucrative arts'. The aim of these taxes was moral and political: to 'ease the poor' and 'throw the burden on the rich', to weaken the incentives for invidious distinction, and to hold back that relentless reproduction of inequality which menaced democratic republicanism. For Rousseau, as for Smith, inequality is the inertial direction of history, 'the natural course of things', but, unlike Smith, he believed it was a course that law and politics could stop: 'It is precisely because the force of circumstances tends continually to destroy equality that the force of legislation should always tend to its maintenance.'[21]

Rousseau's insight is that a community of men can become masters of their needs, instead of slaves to their desires, only when they democratically decide upon some form of collective constraint on inequalities of fortune. These constraints in turn are the necessary economic condition for democracy itself, for the equality of citizens without which there can be no true justice. If this is utopia, Rousseau knew as well as anyone how difficult it would be to achieve:

How many conditions that are difficult to unite does such a government [a democratic republic] pre-suppose! First, a very small state, where the people can readily be got together and where each citizen can with ease know all the rest; secondly, great simplicity of manners, to prevent business from multiplying and raising thorny problems (which would have to be resolved by delegation to experts); next, a larger measure of equality in rank and fortune, without which equality of rights and authority cannot long subsist; lastly, little or no luxury – for luxury either comes of riches or makes them necessary; it corrupts at once rich and poor, the rich by possession and the poor by covetousness; it sells the country to softness and vanity, and takes away from the State all its citizens, to make them slaves one to another, and one and all to public opinion.[22]

Rousseau tried hard to reconcile this utopia, inherited from the 'ancient treatises of virtue', with the modern language of 'commerce and money'. In the *Discourse on Political Economy*, his most extended attempt to ground utopia in an economics of the encircling capitalist world, each new measure of protection against encirclement makes his utopia more coercive. Taxes would have to be levied on both imported and domestic manufactured goods to hold back the tide of luxury, and also to stop the haemorrhage of men and capital from agriculture to commerce, from country to town. The republic would have to ban the importation and production of machines if it wished to prevent unemployment, unrest and the shifting of economic fortunes between classes and between agriculture and industry. Stasis and virtue could only be purchased at the price of liberty.[23]

Rousseau acknowledged that republics without sufficient agricultural resources of their own would have to trade manufactured goods for food. Yet such commerce must be kept to a minimum. International trade only benefits a merchant oligarchy, and in doing so, it menaces the equality of fortune necessary to the maintenance of republican institutions.[24]

Again, Rousseau looked to republican politics to hold back the encircling tide of history. Only if everything changed – if emerging inequality was suppressed by legislative intervention – could everything remain the same.[25] Yet Rousseau realized it was hopeless to look to the direct democracy of citizens to guarantee the insulation of the republic, when some citizens are bound to benefit from trade and luxury. Hence the recurrent appeal in his work to the wise man of virtue, the statesman, who would save the citizens from themselves, who would restore the equality jeopardized by contact with the capitalist order. The republic, in other words, would have to risk even its liberty at the hands of a legislator if it wished to preserve itself against the spiral of need in the capitalist world.

If the republic was menaced from without by the impact of international commerce, it was threatened from within by its citizens' surrender of their civic functions to paid servants of the state.[26] The state bureaucracy would come between the citizen and his duty: a gulf would open up between the private and the public spheres.

The emergence of the modern state, Rousseau argued, was an integral part of the history of need, a necessary consequence of both luxury and inequality. The state emerged to protect the property of the rich against the rapacious envy of the poor, and once in place, it steadily absorbed those functions that private citizens abandoned in their increasing devotion to luxury. The history of the state is therefore part of the history of man's alienation, his loss of a once undivided nature. As men increased their mastery of nature, they chose to delegate tasks like defence to trained specialists – police and standing armies. They did not use their gradual emancipation from natural necessity to expand the range of their natures: they traded away the possibility of virtuous leisure and public participation in the life of the state for the possibility of private gain.[27]

The size of the state grew in step with the amount of time devoted to private economic affairs, and increasing economies in the expenditure of labour time did not increase the time available for civic pursuits: the free time was ploughed back into the pursuit of new means of economizing time and increasing profit. This was the core of Rousseau's answer to the Smithian claim that the productivity of the division of labour not only released people from the burden of basic need, but reduced the time they were required to expend in their satisfaction. These economies of time for Smith were the keys to a historically new type of freedom: the leisure of emancipated desire. Rousseau countered this claim with one of his own: that the free time opened up by modern prosperity was a mirage: it was entirely filled up by delusional pursuit of baubles and trinkets. True freedom lay not in enslavement to what was later to be called 'commodity fetishism' but in participation in the *res publica* of the city-state.

Taken as a whole, Rousseau's writing is the most profound attempt to defend the possibility of an egalitarian republic of citizens within the international division of labour of an emerging capitalist economy. It represents the most sustained attempt any thinker made within the tradition of the 'ancient treatises of morals and virtue' – the Machiavellian moment, as John Pocock has taught us to call this tradition – to argue against the future proposed by the new 'treatises of money and commerce'.

The main burden of Smith's reply to Rousseau, and to the republican language in which he spoke, was to demonstrate that any society which tried to maintain equality and virtue by constraining its needs – chiefly through import duties on luxury goods and taxes on domestic manufactures – would in the end jeopardize the economic growth that ensured the long-term satisfaction of the needs of its poorest members. If growth in productivity depended on the division of labour, and the extent of the division of labour depended in turn on the extent of the market, a republican economy that withdrew as much as possible from the international market and the division of labour would pay the eventual price of stagnation, decline and impoverishment.[28] Those systems of economic policy, both ancient and modern (he was referring to the physiocrats, but also to the ancient republicans) 'which prefering agriculture to all other employments, in order to promote it, impose restraints upon manufactures and foreign trade, act contrary to the very end which they propose.'[29] Prosperous agriculture requires vigorous demand from an urban population dependent upon cash purchase of food.

Inhibiting the growth of the urban manufacturing sector would only hold back the growth of agriculture: it would replace rural depopulation with rural stagnation. The more expensive manufactures were made by taxes and duties, the less of them the farmers would purchase, and the less incentive they would have to produce food. This critique of both republican and physiocratic economics led to a famous Smithian peroration:

All systems either of preference or of restraint therefore being thus completely taken away, the obvious and simple system of natural liberty establishes itself of its own accord. Every man as long as he does not violate the laws of justice is left perfectly free to pursue his own interest his own way, and to bring both his industry and his capital into competition with those of any other man, or order of men.[30]

In place of the republican liberty of laws collectively arrived at, Smith defended the natural liberty of an international market, under the ruthless secular providence of the invisible hand. Smith was convinced that attempts to order 'the natural course of things' by legislation have perverse and unintended effects: perverse because they do not achieve the economic ends intended, and because legislative interference jeopardizes the very liberty of property that republicanism had vowed to defend.

Only a society of strangers, of mediated and indirect social relations, has the dynamism to achieve progress. Only by delegation, specialization, the narrow enclosing of the self in one task, could societies effect the transition from barbarism to civilization.[31] The undivided man of the republican ideal and the communitarian republic were noble but receding temptations, at odds with the reality of a capitalist world.[32]

Characteristically, Smith did not leave the matter there. He worried about the cohesion of a society of strangers so divided by their positions in the division of labour, and divided within themselves, that they could be unable to reconcile their roles as producers and citizens, public and private men.[33] Yet the solution, as far as he was concerned, could only lie in further division of labour: in the formation of a system of education staffed by paid teachers specializing in martial and civic instruction. Only the reproduction of common belief through education could re-forge the social linkages fractured by the division of labour. The invisible hand was evidently no substitute for the allegiances of civic virtue. A market society of strangers lacked the means to know its own general interest as such – hence its unique vulnerability to faction and conflict among economic interests.[34]

Rousseau's solution to the problem – restricting the size of republics so that the identity of interests could be clear to each citizen – may have ignored the existing geography of national states, as well as the logic of international division of labour. Yet the solution proposed by Smith – that of civic education – was no less wishful thinking, a pious gamble on the capacity of strangers to build a common language of civic commitment.

To understand why Rousseau's assessment of the future of civic virtue in commercial society was, in the end, so much more pessimistic than Smith's, we need to return to their fundamental disagreement about the psychology of human sociability. The common threat to virtue in market society, they both agreed, lies in envy and emulation, the desire for invidious distinction that estranges men from themselves and others. In societies without surplus, Rousseau argued, envy was absent. Men were possessed of natural *amour de soi*, a natural self-knowledge and self-regard based in their instinct for self-preservation. This sense of self was autonomous because natural equality deprived the individual of an incentive to compare his satisfactions with those of any other. But with the emergence of surplus, with the emancipation of desire from the limits of universal and equal need, men lost their natural *amour de soi*, and came instead to have a knowledge of self derived from comparison with others. Their identities came to be grounded instead in *amour propre*, in competitive and emulative self-definition against others. In a famous passage from the *Discourse on Inequality* which Smith quoted in his review, Rousseau wrote:

The savage lives in himself; the man of society always out of himself; cannot live but in opinion of others, and it is, if I may say so, from their judgement alone that he derives the sentiment of his own existence.[35]

Men's inner enslavement to the opinions of others grew out of their emerging historical dependence upon each other for subsistence in the division of labour.[36] The pathology of this interdependence was that each man was seized by an 'insatiable ambition, an ardour to raise his relative fortune, not so much from any real necessity, as to set himself above others'. Market relations were thus a theatre of duplicity, in which men served each other's needs only to satisfy their desire of superiority over each other:

To be and to appear to be, became two things entirely different; and from this distinction arose imposing ostentation, deceitful guile and all the vices which attend them.

Smith agreed with Rousseau that 'Nothing tends so much to corrupt and enervate and debase the mind as dependency, and nothing gives such noble and generous notions of probity as freedom and independency.' But for Smith it was precisely in the crucial market transaction – the buying and selling of labour – that the labouring poor had become free to contract for their wages, to leave harsh conditions and seek better ones. It was commerce which had dissolved the dependency relations of patronage, serfdom and clientage of the feudal age.[37]

But what was such freedom worth, Rousseau might well have replied, if the poor had no desires but those of the rich, if they had no way of distinguishing needs from fetishes? What anyone else desires, the self desires by that very fact. Yet this neglected, Smith insisted, the human capacity for self-command and self-detachment. Men were capable of distinguishing between their *amour propre* and their *amour de soi*, and they could act accordingly, keeping a virtuous detachment from the 'great scramble of human society'.[38] And what the 'wise and virtuous few' could do, humans in general could do.

This is a language of the will, a Stoic's language – yet it turns Stoic premises against one of Stoicism's most ardent advocates. For as many scholars have pointed out, the Stoic definition of man as a creature distinguished not by his passions but by his will ordered all of Rousseau's thought.[39] As he wrote in the *Discourse on Inequality*, 'Nature lays her command on every animal and the brute obeys her voice. Man receives the same impulsion but at the same time knows himself at liberty to acquiesce or desist.'[40] Indeed, it was only in the social world of men that this capacity to choose the good, instead of merely following natural instinct, could exercise itself.[41] In the language we have been using, man becomes himself only when he can choose between what he needs and what he desires.

Rousseau's account of how men enslave themselves to the spiral of needs is the first specifically modern theory of false consciousness, the first to take the ancient Stoic account of moral corruption and link it to the economic conditions of modern capitalist society – inequality, acquisitive envy and the division of labour. Smith's reply is paradigmatic of all critiques of false consciousness since: if men are creatures of will, they can choose; if they can choose, they can keep their distances from the 'great scramble of society' by learning to judge their own conduct from the vantage point of an impartial spectator.[42]

The encounter between Rousseau and Smith in 1756 offers the most fundamental legacy of political choice bequeathed to the nineteenth century, and through it to us, by the Enlightenment. It is a choice between two languages about politics, and two different utopias. We must say utopia in both cases, because Smith's 'system of natural liberty' no more described the world as it was than did Rousseau's republican ideal.

Rousseau's utopia is a republic of needs, a society which by democratically limiting its size, its contact with the world outside, and most of all, the domestic consumption of its citizens, reduces inequality, envy and competition. It constrains desire within a set of democratic limits of need, and it does so for the sake of social solidarity, civic virtue, and the primacy of public over private life. It does so at a cost. Societies that constrain the economic desires of their citizens, that guard their political integrity within an international division of labour by autarky, and that try to make the distribution of wealth and income a matter of collective choice, risk economic stagnation. They risk becoming unable to meet the first requirement of a just society: that it satisfy the basic needs of all. Moreover, the apparatus of constraints on individual desire, necessary to restrain inequality and to promote civic virtue, potentially jeopardizes the liberty which is the republic's *raison d'être*.

As Rousseau understood, citizens can only be free in a republic of need if the constraints to which each submits are willed and chosen by each. Less *is* more in such a society only if each citizen gives his consent. Such a republic requires heroic displays of stoic self-command by each citizen: each individual, to remain truly free, must consent, in the deepest recesses of his self, to the yoke of collectively determined constraints upon desire; each must refuse the temptation that passion offers to desire more than one's fellow citizens. Rousseau held out hope that the experience of civic equality itself would remove the temptation to compete. Virtue would become natural, that is, fully social, because society should remove the incentives for envy. He did not seek to hide the intense demands which his utopia would make of the civic virtue of its citizens. Were they to relax their guard, were they to entrust the choice of virtue to others, were they to renounce their sovereignty, both over their own passions and over their polity, the republic would surrender its freedom. It would terminate in a dictatorship of need.

If Rousseau speaks for a republic of needs, Smith envisages

the society of the future as a collectivity whose economic dynamic is the unlimited expansion of desire. Neither natural scarcity nor satiation of desire was ever likely, Smith argued, to limit either the spiral of human desire for commodities or the capacity of the system to deliver.[43] To the degree that he anticipated the problem of Malthusian limits on the expansion of a commercial economy Smith dismissed them by means of the division of labour argument.[44] As long as productivity per man hour could be kept rising in step with population, and the market could continue to expand to embrace the whole planet, these demographic and ecological constraints could be pushed back indefinitely. The specific historical property of a commercial society, he insisted, was that it was no longer threatened by the cycle of expansion and decline that had brought earlier modes of subsistence, earlier empires, to their term, for the extension of the division of labour to the world market made permanent economic expansion possible for the first time in human history.[45] The fourth stage – commercial society – was thus the last stage of historical time, the apotheosis of a history of progress that had begun in the mists of the past among the first hunters and gatherers.

A market society was not threatened by stagnation and backwardness but it was menaced by the features which a republic could avoid: inequality, envy and competition. A capitalist society might trade public liberty for private liberty, active citizenship for private, passive freedom to enjoy one's property.[46] In this sense, if the freedom of a republic of needs risked degenerating into a dictatorship of needs, the freedom of market society risked degenerating into a despotism of the rich.

In the end, Smith had to make demands on the virtue of this utopia's participants as austere as Rousseau's. A market society could remain free and virtuous only if all its citizens were capable of stoic self-command. Without this self-command, competition would become a deluded scramble, politics a war of factions, and government a dictatorship of the rich. Smith was optimistic, but it was an optimism based on a stoic hope that the human will would prevail, and each individual would retain the capacity to know the difference between what he wants and what he needs.

After Rousseau, the greatest modern attempt to explain how we might become capable of choosing our needs within a civic community is in the work of Marx.[47] His vision of a communist future began from a libertarian assumption shared indeed with Smith: no society of the future ought to constrain the needs of its members. A dictatorship of needs would confine human development within the cage of 'crude communism' and enforced equality at a static and barbarous level.[48]

The task of human progress was to increase the productivity of labour so that all human beings could be freed from the slavery of basic need to embrace the free choice of desire. In capitalist society, the rising productivity of labour had freed the poorest from basic need at the price of enslaving them to wage labour and commodity fetishism: only the rich and propertied enjoyed the liberation from labour promised by progress. Like Aristotle, like all philosophers of classical citizenship, Marx believed that human beings could become citizens, could transcend the gulf between private and public existence and recover their full human capacities, their 'species being', only if they enjoyed leisure and the free determination of time.[49]

How then was the alienating upward spiral of commodity fetishism and wage labour to be broken so that all men could become citizens again? Marx believed a communist society could, by placing the means of production under collective ownership and by directing them to satisfy all unmet needs in the population, release the productive capacities of modern industry held in check by wasteful consumption, competition and misallocation of capital under private property relations. Indeed, the moral and historical necessity of socialist revolution rested, especially in Marx's *Grundrisse*, on the proposition that capitalist production was reaching the limits of its capacity to reduce labour time and satisfy commodity needs.[50] Once released from their capitalist fetters, the means of production under socialism would become so efficient that all outstanding commodity needs would be satisfied, and the labour time necessary for their production would be progressively reduced.

In the fantastic if barbarous productivity of the modern capitalist order, Marx believed, there existed an engine to create a new utopia which could transcend the constraints on private consumption, the disdain for 'luxury' at the heart of the ancient republican ideal. Like Rousseau, Marx assumed in effect that the privatizing and competitive addiction to luxury – to material consumption – was a consequence of social scarcity in conditions of class inequality. Overcome inequality and raise the productivity of labour, and all men's relative and absolute needs for commodities could be satisfied. In the plenitude of material satisfaction, the old antithesis between the claims of private interest and public good would be transcended: men's desiring would shift naturally from the material realm to the higher realms of moral and intellectual cultivation and socialist public spiritedness.

This attempt to reconcile the productivist vision of Smith with the political vision of Rousseau wished away the conflict between human needs which the ancient utopian ideal at least had the courage to recognize. Our needs are not complementary: the needs we have for family, home, and private belonging, conflict with the needs we have for public belonging. The ancient republican vision recognized this conflict and made stoic will the core of political virtue. In the socialist paradise of unlimited self-development, essential conflicts between needs are wished away in the fantasy of productivist plenitude.

The core of the Marxian project was to provide a destination for the tragic spiral of need. Communism is a myth of plenitude at the end of time. When, in his most Promethean moment of enthusiasm, Marx said that Communism was the solution to the riddle of history and knew it to be such, he meant, among other things, that it was the state of Paradise beyond the tragic dialectic between human need and human labour.

If on Marx's own assumptions, however, human needs are intrinsically dynamic, it is unlikely either that saturation of outstanding demand for commodities will occur or that the spiral of human needing will transfer its energies from the sphere of commodities to the sphere of self-cultivation. In many ways, Smith and Rousseau were more consistent in facing up to the implication that human needing is historical. Smith's vision of progress contained no myth of future deliverance, no fantasy of human self-transcendence through the mastery of the means of production. Progress delivered only one ambiguous good: increasing the freedom of individuals to choose between need and desire. It could not promise a future in which men would be relieved of the burden of stoic choice.

Marx's thesis of the inevitability and universality of world revolution also enabled him to side-step the crucial question of how a self-governing community can master its needs in an international economy. No matter how insistently he claimed that the vision of world revolution was grounded in the sober inevitability of political economy and crisis theory, it was a fantasy of deliverance from history that owed a suppressed debt to the religious image of the apocalypse.

A hundred years later, the societies whose revolutions were inspired by this vision of liberation from history have become the dystopias of our time. 'Actually existing socialism' has vanquished natural scarcity, but at the cost of increasing relative or social scarcity through the institution of the party *nomenklatura* and its privileges. Having abolished the antagonism of classes based on differential access to property, they have reproduced a new antagonism of classes based on differential access to state power. They are societies as materialist in their common vocabulary of aspiration as any in the West. Indeed, by a perverse irony, the actually existing abundance of Western capitalist society has

become the utopia for many inhabitants of actually existing socialism.

This ironic and tragic enactment of utopia is an endless source
of self-congratulation in the West. Yet where in this global
empire, in this universal market that prides itself on reconciling
economic progress and political freedom, *are* the polities that are
truly masters of their societies' needs? Only a handful of nations
have succeeded in achieving any degree of control over the terms
of their dependency on the international economy. In scores of
the former colonies which have tried to enact the dreams of
self-determination their European masters taught them, the passage from colonial status in an imperial preference zone to nation-
hood in a brutal international market has actually reduced their
capacity to meet their people's basic needs. Where once their
agriculture was sufficiently diversified to feed their populations,
now their economies depend dangerously on monocultures, on
the export of cash crops or basic resources in return for international currency.[51] As a result, their people are ever more
dependent on the cruel arbiters of international trade – exchange
rates and world commodity prices.

In the free-trade utopia of eighteenth-century political economy, poor nations were supposed to climb towards the economic
strength necessary to national self-determination by exploiting
the comparative advantage of their cheap labour in the international market.[52] In practice, only the imperial powers themselves, the rich nations, have managed to realize the ideals of
autonomy, independence and economic mastery implied in this
classical model of an international economy. The republican
dream of economic and national independence has required
all the violence and domination of imperial power in order to
come true.

Thus by a paradox that Smith was the first to understand fully,
the economy in which our needs are now satisfied has become
global while the polity in which we try to control the pace and

development of these needs remains national. Not even the great imperial powers can escape the challenge to their sovereignty presented by the global invisible hand. In a world market, where the balance of comparative advantage and the relative pricing of scarce factors of production constantly shift, the only power which really counts in a capitalist economy – the power to predict the future – is decisively limited. The metaphor of the invisible hand implies as much: knowledge of its determination of our destiny can be had only retrospectively; prospectively its operations are unknowable.

The global economy is a human institution and as the great eighteenth-century historiographer Giambattista Vico told us, what man himself has made man can understand and control.[53] This was the heroic charter of classical political economy, indeed of all eighteenth-century social science. Yet the order which our science is now called upon to understand is an order of strangers extending to the ends of the earth; it is an order in which so innocent an act of consumption here in London as the making of a cup of tea implicates us in the oppression of tea workers in the British plantations in Bangladesh and Sri Lanka.

Smith's confidence in the civilizing mission of the invisible hand tacitly assumed an imperial order which would keep the global market under its sovereignty. His concluding chapters on the dispute with the American colonies envisaged a federated imperium, reconciling the claims of colonial independence with British imperial predominance in the world market. The multipolar world which the invisible hand has brought to pass will no longer submit to any one imperium: the scramble for competitive advantage has been universalized and no one economic power has the leverage to submit the scramble to its rules. Economy has broken away from the reins of polity.

In such a world, the language of the common good which we inherited from the noblest classical language of politics, guides us imperfectly. In that language, the public good was the good of the city. The common responsibilities of citizenship ebbed away at the city gates: beyond were the barbarians. Yet for at least two hundred years, since the *Wealth of Nations*, we have known that the cities we happen to be born in depend for the satisfaction of their needs on the labour and resources of strangers stretched across the expanse of the globe. The partition of sovereignties and obligations tacitly implied in the classical language of republican politics is no longer possible for us. Today, the price of that highest of the ancient republican virtues – patriotism – would be the destruction of all cities. Today, the unintended consequences of our consumption choices within the city gates are visited on the whole ecology of the globe. We have inherited a language of political allegiance which no longer speaks for the needs we have, not as citizens, but as members of a common species.

Yet – and with this we return to Lear, to the 'poor, bare, forked animal' – it is doubtful that our sense of identity as members of a species is strong enough to overcome our sense of identity based on difference. We are the first generation to have seen our planet under the gaze of eternity, not from this mountain top or that city tower, but from an astronaut's window, revolving mist-wrapped in the cobalt darkness of space. We are the first generation to have lived under the shared threat of ecological and nuclear catastrophe. Progress, the passage from savagery to civilization, now conveys us towards apocalypse, the end of time. That tragic history of need, of which Smith and Rousseau were the great visionaries, has finally made us one: every part of the planet is now subject to the spiralling dialectic of need and human labour, and every part of the planet is under the same threat of extinction. Yet – and this is the truth before which thinking about politics has stalled – the more evident our common needs as a species become, the more brutal becomes the human insistence on the claims of difference. The centripetal forces of need, labour and science which are pulling us together as a species are counter-balanced by centrifugal forces, the claims of tribe, race, class, section, region and nation, pulling us apart.

Millions of people have perished since 1945 in the wars, revolutions and civil strife safely conducted under the umbrella of a nuclear peace, under the watching gaze of our imperial policemen. Most of this dying has been in the name of freedom, in the name of liberation from a colonial, tribal, religious or racial oppressor. It is a waste of breath to press the claims of common human identity on men and women prepared to die in defence of their claims of difference. There will be no end to the dying, and no time for the claim of our common species being, until each people is safe within its borders, with a sovereignty which makes them master of their needs. Only when difference has its home, when the need for belonging in all its murderous intensity has been assuaged, can our common identity begin to find its voice.

CONCLUSION: HOMELESSNESS AND BELONGING

Modernity is the transient, the fleeting,
the contingent; it is one half of art, the other being
the eternal and the immovable.

BAUDELAIRE

I ask around all Paris, for it's
only in stories or pictures
that people rise to the skies:
where is your soul gone, where?

TSVETAYEVA

It seems a fact of life that individuals have different needs. Some people need religious consolation, while others do not; some need citizenship, while others seem content with a purely private existence; some pursue riches, while others pursue knowledge, power, sex, even danger. Who is to say which is the truer path to human fulfilment? If human nature is historical, individuals have different histories and therefore different needs.

If this is all we can say about human needs, then it seems to follow that the proper domain of politics ought to be the satisfaction of people's expressed desires, rather than the enactment of some vision of what their needs might be. A free society can stand for justice – for the idea that private preferences should not result in harm to others – but if it stands for more than justice, it will jeopardize the freedom of individuals to choose their needs as they see fit.

This is the core of the liberal creed in politics. It draws a line between the needs which can be made a matter of public entitlement and those which must be left to the private self to satisfy. Since the disestablishment of the churches and the granting of rights of toleration, some of our most durable historical needs – for consolation and ultimate explanation – have passed into the domain of private choice. Likewise, a market society leaves it up to each of us to find work capable of satisfying our needs for purpose and meaning. By and large, few of us would exchange the freedom to choose our own beliefs and our own vocation for the solidarity of the Islamic or Stalinist theocracies of the modern age.

Doubtless the price of our freedom to choose our needs is high. We have Augustine's freedom to choose, and because we do, we cannot have the second freedom, the certainty of having chosen rightly. That certainty, Augustine believed, could only be granted by the gift of Grace. The modern political utopias of Rousseau and Marx were attempts to imagine a secular political equivalent to the state of Grace, a state of social unity in which each private self would feel its own choices ordered and confirmed by the general will. As such, their resolution of the alienation between self and society was a leap out of politics into metaphysics. If this is where our needs for certainty take us, it would be better for us to be reconciled to the burdens of our private choosing.

Yet the problem they posed remains. Is there a form of society which could reconcile freedom and solidarity? Is there a society which would allow each of us to choose our needs as we see fit, while providing us with the necessary means to make these choices? Freedom is empty as long as we are trapped in physical necessity. Freedom is also empty if we lack a language in which we can choose the good.

For all its many shortcomings the modern welfare state can be understood as an attempt to reconcile these antinomies: to create a society in which individuals would be given what they need so that they would be free to choose the good. For all the apparent relativism of liberal society – our interminable debate about what the good in politics consists in – in practice a shared good is administered in our name by the welfare bureaucracies of the modern state. From birth, our needs for health and welfare, education and employment are defined for us by doctors, social workers, lawyers, public health inspectors, school principals – experts in the administration of needs.

The paradox is that this continuous intrusion into the logic of our own choosing has been legitimized by our public commitment to freedom of choice. It has been in order to equalize everyone's chances at a free life that the state now meets needs for food, shelter, clothing, education, transport and health care (at least in some countries). It is in the name of freedom that experts in need now pronounce on the needs of strangers. Apparently, societies that seek to give everyone the same chance at freedom can only do so at some cost to freedom itself.

This is not the only irony. One might have expected that the enactment of a vision of the shared good in the welfare state would have brought us closer together. The welfare state has tried to enact fraternity by giving each individual a claim of right to common resources. Yet meeting everyone's basic needs does not necessarily meet their needs for social solidarity. Equalized social provision does not seem to reduce competition: it redoubles the scramble for scarce status goods.[1]

In the welfare state, old divisions of class have been re-expressed as divisions between those dependent on the state, and those free to satisfy their needs in the market-place. Welfare dependency is still scarred with stigma. Up to a point, a welfare society can reduce these divisions by trying to guarantee that public goods are as attractive as private ones, and by limiting the rights of the wealthy to opt out of public provision in such fields as education and health care. It is not clear that abolishing the right of the wealthy to opt out will end the debate between the claims of liberty and the claims of equality. In any society we can imagine, these goods are in conflict, and the cost of conflict is necessarily measured in solidarity and fraternity.

It is a recurring temptation in political argument to suppose that these conflicts can be resolved in principle, to believe that we can rank human needs in an order of priority which will avoid dispute. Yet who really knows whether we need freedom more than we need solidarity, or fraternity more than equality? Modern secular humanism is empty if it supposes that the human good is without internal contradiction. These contradictions cannot be resolved in principle, only in practice.

A language of needs cannot reconcile our contradictory goods; it can only help us to say what they are. The problem is that our language is not necessarily adequate to our needs.

Language which has ceased to express felt needs is empty rhetoric. Much of our language carries a heavy legacy of past attachments and commitments: it is always an open question whether we genuinely share these commitments or are simply mouthing the platitudes which are their sign.

Needs which lack a language adequate to their expression do not simply pass out of speech: they may cease to be felt. The generations that have grown up without ever hearing the language of religion may not feel the slightest glimmer of a religous need. If our needs are historical, they can have a beginning and an end, and their end arrives when the words for their expression begin to ring hollow in our ears.

Of all the needs I have mentioned the one which raises this problem of the adequacy of language in its acutest form is the need for fraternity, social solidarity, for civic belonging. Needs can only live when the language which expresses them is adequate to the times. Words like fraternity, belonging and community are so soaked with nostalgia and utopianism that they are nearly useless as guides to the real possibilities of solidarity in modern society. Modern life has changed the possibilities of civic solidarity, and our language stumbles behind like an overburdened porter with a mountain of old cases.

Right up to the First World War, the very idea of being a citizen, of belonging to a society or a nation would have seemed a distant abstraction to the peasants who made up the majority of the European population. Such belonging as a peasant felt was bounded by the distances his legs could walk and his cart could roll. Until 1914, most European peasants spoke in regional dialects; national languages were apparatuses of state rather than the living speech of those they administered. It was only as the school, the medical officer and the census taker – the institutions of the national state – began to permeate the village world that the nation became a living entity and national belonging became a felt need of millions. With the mass mobilization of the European peasantry in August 1914, modern nationalism found its voice and the need for belonging finally spoke in the cries for war which resounded around Europe. In those cries, the other possible belonging – the internationale of working men of all nations – was swept aside like a pile of leaflets in the wind.[2]

A century of total war has taught us where belonging can take us when its object is the nation. Out of that experience, it is just possible that our need is taking a new form, finding a new object: the fragile green and blue earth itself, the floating disk we are the first generation to see from space. No generation has ever understood the common nature of our fate more deeply, and out of that understanding may be born a real identification, not with this country or that, but with the earth itself. Of course this seems fanciful, but that is just my point. Modernity is changing the locus of belonging: our language of attachments limps suspiciously behind, doubting that our needs could ever find larger attachments. Already, however, we can just begin to feel our old attachments, our old citizenship, being emptied of its rationale. All the changes which impinge upon the politics of modern states are global in character: the market in which we trade, and in which our economic futures will be shaped, is global; the ecology in which we live and breathe is global. The political life of nation states is being emptied of relevance by the inconsequence and impotence of national sovereignties. People's attachment to nations depends on their belief that the nation is the relevant arbiter of their private fate. This is less and less so. Political languages which appeal to us only as citizens of a nation, and never as common inhabitants of the earth, may find themselves abandoned by those in search of a truer expression of their ultimate attachments.

Our task is to find a language for our need for belonging which is not just a way of expressing nostalgia, fear and estrangement from modernity. Our political images of civic belonging remain haunted by the classical *polis*, by Athens, Rome and Florence. Is there a language of belonging adequate to Los Angeles? Put like that the answer can only seem to be no. Yet we should remember the nineteenth-century city and the richness of its invention of new forms and possibilities of belonging. Those great cities – Manchester, New York, Paris – were as strange to those who had to live in them for the first time as ours may seem to us. Yet we look back at them now as a time of civic invention – the boulevard, the public park, the museum, the café, the trolley car, street lighting, the subway, the railway, the apartment house. Each of these humble institutions created a new possibility for fraternity among strangers in public places.

It was in literature and painting rather than in political language that the possibilities of urban belonging were first given adequate images. Think of Gogol's evocation of the proximity of loneliness and happiness on the Nevsky Prospekt in the 1850s, think of Baudelaire's *flâneur* and the intense society of Haussmann's boulevards, of Toulouse-Lautrec's bars and bordellos, Degas's circus crowds, and Seurat's bathers at Neuilly, each couple sitting separately by the water's edge, alone and yet together, sharing civic space in the silence of the painter's eye. In these images of civic life, loneliness and belonging, togetherness and estrange-ment live cheek by jowl; every exchanged glance, every instant of pleasure, is tinged with portents of loss.[3]

Edward Hopper belongs to this tradition, inventing a new language of painting to express the silent closeness of strangers in the city. Think of the usherette resting her feet in the darkened aisle of the movie theatre, alone at the edge of a sea of watching faces; the woman sunning herself in the window of the apartment just across the fire-escape; the nighthawks in the diner in the cube of warmth and light sheltering them from darkness. In all these pictures, there is always one pair of eyes sharing the solitude of these figures, one absent presence: our own. Hopper's work is an image of our own impingement on the lives of strangers.

If it seems puzzling to think of these as images of belonging, it is because our language has not caught up with modernity. We think of belonging as permanence, yet all our homes are transient. Who still lives in the house of their childhood? Who still lives in the neighbourhood where they grew up? Home is the place we have to leave in order to grow up, to become ourselves. We think of belonging as rootedness in a small familiar place, yet home for most of us is the convulsive arteries of a great city. Our belonging is no longer to something fixed, known and familiar, but to an electric and heartless creature eternally in motion.

We think of belonging in moral terms as direct impingement on the lives of others: fraternity implies the closeness of brothers. Yet the moral relations that exist between my income and the needs of strangers at my door pass through the arteries of the state.

Perhaps above all we think of belonging as the end of yearning itself, as a state of rest and reconciliation with ourselves beyond need itself. Yet modernity and insatiability are inseparable.

It is the painters and writers, not the politicians or the social scientists, who have been able to find a language for the joy of modern life, its fleeting and transient solidarity. It is Hopper's images of New York, Joyce's Dublin, Musil's Vienna, Bellow's Chicago, Kundera's Prague, which take us beyond easy laments about the alienation of modern life, which have enabled us to find a language for the new pleasures of living as we do.

We need justice, we need liberty, and we need as much solidarity as can be reconciled with justice and liberty. But we also need, as much as anything else, language adequate to the times we live in. We need to see how we live now and we can only see with words and images which leave us no escape into nostalgia for some other time and place.

We need words to keep us human. Being human is an accomplishment like playing an instrument. It takes practice. The keys must be mastered. The old scores must be committed to memory. It is a skill we can forget. A little noise can make us forget the notes. The best of us is historical; the best of us is fragile. Being human is a second nature which history taught us, and which terror and deprivation can batter us into forgetting.

Our needs are made of words: they come to us in speech, and they can die for lack of expression. Without a public language to help us find our own words, our needs will dry up in silence. It is words only, the common meanings they bear, which give me the right to speak in the name of the strangers at my door. Without a language adequate to this moment we risk losing ourselves in resignation towards the portion of life which has been allotted to us. Without the light of language, we risk becoming strangers to our better selves:

> We are brothers, we are brothers?
> ... if these things are true, they
> are perfectly simple, perfectly
> impenetrable, those primary elements
> which can only be named.
> GEORGE OPPEN

NOTES

INTRODUCTION: TRAGEDY AND UTOPIA

1 – On the relation between needs and rights, see Raymond Plant, Harry Lesser and Peter Taylor-Gooby *Political Philosophy and Social Welfare: Essays on the Normative Basis of Welfare Provision* (London: Routledge and Kegan Paul, 1980), ch. 2; see also David Miller *Social Justice* (Oxford: Clarendon Press, 1976); Jonathan Bradshaw 'The Concept of Social Need', *New Society*, 30 March 1972, pp. 640–643; Ian Gough *The Political Economy of the Welfare State* (London: Macmillan, 1979).
2 – John Rawls *A Theory of Justice* (Oxford: Clarendon Press, 1972), p. 92.
3 – Ivan Illich *Towards a History of Needs* (New York: Pantheon, 1978).
4 – One recent attempt to write a history of need as an idea is Patricia Springborg *The Problem of Human Needs and the Critique of Civilization* (London: George Allen and Unwin, 1981). It attempts to make a continuous history out of the idea of need from the Stoics through to Marxism and psychoanalysis – for example Marcuse and Fromm; most of the other recent work on needs takes the form of a commentary and critique on Marx. See for example, Kate Soper *On Human Needs: Open and Closed Theories in a Marxist Perspective* (Brighton: Harvester, 1981; Atlantic Highlands, NJ: Humanities Press, 1981); Agnes Heller *The Theory of Need in Marx* (London: Allison and Busby, 1976); see also William Leiss *The Limits to Satisfaction: An Essay on the Problem of Needs and Commodities* (Toronto: University of Toronto Press, 1976).

CHAPTER 1 · THE NATURAL AND THE SOCIAL

1 – An important attempt to develop a language of entitlements for the case of famine is Amartya Sen *Poverty and Famines: An Essay on Entitlement and Deprivation* (Oxford: Clarendon Press, 1981); see also Peter Singer *Practical Ethics* (Cambridge: Cambridge University Press, 1979), ch. 8.
2 – In writing this essay on *King Lear*, I learned most from three recent performances, and a memory of a fourth: Jonathan Miller's production for the BBC, the RSC production with Michael Gambon as Lear,

directed by Adrian Noble; Laurence Olivier's Lear; and the memory, perhaps most important of all, of Peter Brook and Paul Scofield's production. I also learned a great deal about the arts of acting Shakespeare from a conversation with Patrick Stewart of the RSC. I also want to express my indebtedness to Marvin Rosenberg's *The Masks of King Lear* (Berkeley: University of California, 1972), a brilliant study of the history of the play's production and performance; see also Janet Adelman (ed:) *Twentieth Century Interpretations of King Lear: A Collection of Critical Essays* (Englewood Cliffs, NJ: Prentice Hall, 1978); Frank Kermode (ed.) *King Lear: A Casebook* (London: Macmillan, 1978).

3 – Stanley Cavell 'The Avoidance of Love' in his *Must We Mean What We Say?* (Cambridge: University Press, 1976), pp. 272–300.

4 – On the Elizabethan heath and the masterless man, see Christopher Hill *The Century of Revolution, 1603–1714* (Edinburgh: Nelson, 1961); also his *Society and Puritanism in Pre-Revolutionary England* (London: Panther, 1979); R. H. Tawney *Religion and the Rise of Capitalism* (London: Penguin, 1966), 'The New Medicine for Poverty', pp. 251–271; also his *The Agrarian Problem in the Sixteenth Century* (New York: Harper, 1967).

5 – This theme is, of course, the central contention of Michel Foucault's *Madness and Civilization: A History of Insanity in the Age of Reason* (New York: Vintage, 1973).

6 – My first book, *A Just Measure of Pain: The Penitentiary in the Industrial Revolution, 1750–1850* (New York: Pantheon, 1978; London: Macmillan, 1979; Milan: Mondadori, 1981) was about the historical invention of the prison as a place for the re-making of souls. The classic account of the 'total institution' as a moral world is Erving Goffman *Asylums* (Garden City, NJ: Doubleday Anchor, 1961); for an insightful treatment of the human rights problems of prisoners and other inmates see David A. Richards 'Rights, Utility and Crime' in *Crime and Justice: An Annual Review of Research*, vol. 3 (Chicago: University of Chicago Press, 1981), pp. 247–295.

7 – See, for example, the United Nations Declaration of Human Rights, 1948, and the commentary and critique in D. D. Raphael *Political Theory and the Rights of Man* (London: Macmillan, 1967).

CHAPTER 2 · BODY AND SPIRIT

1 – Augustine, Bishop of Hippo *Concerning the City of God Against the Pagans* (London: Penguin, 1972), Book XIV.

2 – Augustine, Bishop of Hippo *Confessions* (London: Penguin, 1961), Book VIII, ch. 8.

3 – *Confessions*, VIII, 9; *City of God*, XIV, 16.

4 – *City of God*, XIV, 3.

5 – *City of God*, XIV, 19.

6 – *Confessions*, III, 1.

7 – Peter Brown *Augustine of Hippo: a Biography* (London: Faber and Faber, 1967), p. 374. My debt to this book and to the author's other works on the history of religion should be obvious. See also his *The Cult of the Saints: Its Rise and Function in Latin Christianity* (London: SCM Press, 1981); also *Religion and Society in the Age of Saint Augustine* (London: Faber and Faber, 1972).

8 – Lucius Annaeus Seneca *Letters from a Stoic* (London: Penguin, 1969), p. 65; Anthony A. Long *Hellenistic Philosophy: Stoics, Epicureans, Sceptics* (London: Duckworth, 1974), pp. 174–5; Patricia Springborg *The Problem of Human Needs and the Critique of Civilization* (London: George Allen and Unwin, 1981), pp. 19–21. On Augustinian doctrine of the will, see also Bishop Augustine *On Free Choice of the Will* (Indianapolis: Bobbs Merrill, 1964).

9 – Quoted in Brown *Augustine*, pp. 374–5.

10 – R. L. Delevoy *Bosch* (Cleveland: Skira, 1960).

11 – Walter S. Gibson *Hieronymus Bosch* (London: Thames and Hudson, 1973), p. 16.

12 – Thomas à Kempis *The Imitation of Christ* (London: Penguin, 1980).

13 – *Confessions*, X, 31.

14 – Carl Linfert, *Hieronymus Bosch: The Paintings* (London: Phaidon Press, 1959), p. 23.

15 – Wilhelm Franger *The Millennium of Hieronymus Bosch* (London: Faber and Faber, 1952); see also John Rowlands *The Garden of Earthly Delights* (Oxford: Phaidon, 1979); P. S. Beagle *The Garden of Earthly Delights* (London: Secker and Warburg, 1982).

16 – On the Pelagian heresy, see Peter Brown *Religion and Society in the Age of Saint Augustine*, pp. 195–199; there is a helpful discussion on the medieval and early modern continuation of the Pelagian–Augustinian controversy on grace, will and works in A. H. T. Levi's introduction to the Penguin edition of Erasmus *Praise of Folly* (London: Penguin, 1971), especially pp. 18–22.

17 – Saint Thomas Aquinas *Summa Theologica*, I^e-II^{ac}Q.82, Art. 3; see *Nature and Grace: Selections from the Summa Theologica* (London: Library of Christian Classics, vol. XI, 1954).

18 – Aquinas *Summa Theologica*, Iª-IIªᶜ, Q. 4; see the collection *Philosophical Texts* (London: Oxford University Press, 1962).

19 – Desiderius Erasmus *Praise of Folly and Letter to Martin Dorp* (London: Penguin, 1971), pp. 207–208; for a delightful and masterly study of the theme of Christian folly see M. A. Screech *Ecstasy and the Praise of Folly* (London: Duckworth, 1980).

20 – Blaise Pascal *Pensées* (London: Penguin, 1966), p. 309; see also Alban Krailsheimer *Pascal* (Oxford: Oxford University Press, 1980); Lucien Goldman *The Hidden God: A Study of Tragic Vision in the Pensées of Pascal and the Tragedies of Racine* (London: Routledge and Kegan Paul, 1964), p. 170. On Pascal's politics, see N. O. Keohane *Philosophy and the State in France: the Renaissance to the Enlightenment* (Princeton: Princeton University Press, 1980); for the contrast between the God of reasoners and the God of mystics, see Leszek Kolakowski *Religion* (Glasgow: Fontana, 1982), chs. 2–3.

21 – On the connection between Jansenism and Augustinianism see Anthony Levi *French Moralists: The Theory of the Passions* (Oxford: Clarendon Press, 1964); on faith and reason in Pascal, see L. Kolakowski, *Religion*, pp. 204–6; A. Krailsheimer, *Pascal*, passim.

22 – Pascal *Pensées*, pp. 155–164.

CHAPTER 3 · METAPHYSICS AND THE MARKET

1 – James Boswell *Boswell in Extremes, 1776–1778* (New Haven: Yale University Press, 1971), pp. 11–15.

2 – David Hume 'Autobiography' in *Essays, Moral, Political and Literary*, 2 vols. (London: Longmans, Green, 1875), vol. 1, p. 7.

3 – Adam Smith *Correspondence* (Oxford: Oxford University Press, 1977), pp. 203–4, 218; on Lucian's influence on modern European satirical traditions see Christopher Robinson *Lucian and his Influence in Europe* (London: Duckworth, 1979).

4 – Smith *Correspondence*, pp. 203–4, 218.

5 – Smith *Correspondence*, pp. 210–211.

6 – Smith *Correspondence*, pp. 217–221.

7 – George Horne, Bishop of Norwich *A Letter to Adam Smith* (Oxford: 1777), pp. 9–10.

8 – *Boswell in Extremes*, p. 270.

9 – Hume, *Essays*, vol. 2, p. 108.

10 – *Boswell in Extremes*, p. 114.

11 – David Hume *The Letters of David Hume*, 2 vols. (Oxford: Clarendon Press, 1932), vol. 1, pp. 32–3.

12 – David Hume *Enquiries Concerning Human Understanding and Concerning the Principles of Morals* (Oxford: Oxford University Press, 1975), p. 11; see also Anthony Flew *Hume's Philosophy of Belief: A Study of his First Inquiry* (London: Routledge and Kegan Paul, 1960) pp. 1–22.

13 – David Hume *A Treatise of Human Nature* (Oxford: Oxford University Press, 1978), p. 264; see also Nicholas Phillipson 'Hume as Moralist: a Social Historian's Perspective', unpublished paper, University of Edinburgh History Dept., 1978.

14 – E. C. Mossner, *The Life of David Hume* (Oxford: Clarendon Press, 1980), p. 70; on the theme of the hidden God in seventeenth-century French thought, see. L. Goldman *The Hidden God*, pp. 50–57.

15 – Hume *Treatise*, p. 269.

16 – Hume *Enquiries*, p. 159.

17 – Mossner *Life of Hume*, ch. 1; Anon *The Whole Duty of Man* (London: 1658). I used the 1841 London edition.

18 – Pascal *Pensées*, pp. 155–164 on the theme of diversion. On the influence of Jansenist thought on economic philosophy in France in the eighteenth century, see J. C. Perrot 'La Main Invisible et le dieu Caché' in his *Mélanges en l'honneur de Louis Dumont* (Paris, 1983).

19 – Pierre Bayle *Selections from Bayle's Dictionary* (Princeton: Princeton University Press, 1952); see also Elizabeth Labrousse's excellent essay *Bayle* (Oxford: Oxford University Press, 1983), pp. 49–60. The quotation comes from Bayle's article on Spinoza in the Dictionary. On Hume's contact with Bayle's thought, see J. P. Pittion 'Hume's Study of Bayle: An Inquiry into the Source and Role of the Memorandum', *Journal of the History of Philosophy*, 15, 1977, pp. 373–386.

20 – Hume *Enquiries*, p. 160. Nicolas de Malebranche *De la recherche de la vérité* in *Oeuvres*, 2 vols., vol. 1 (Paris: Gallimard, 1979), Book V, ch. 2.

21 – Hume *Treatise*, p. 486.

22 Hume *Essays*, vol. 2, p. 104 ('The Sceptic').

23 – Hume *Essays*, vol. 1, p. 229, n. 12.

24 – Adam Smith *The Theory of Moral Sentiments* (Oxford: Oxford University Press, 1976), III.3.30. Hereafter cited as TMS.

25 – Hume *Treatise*, pp. 413–418.

26 – Adam Smith *Lectures on Jurisprudence* (Oxford: Oxford University Press, 1978); hereafter known as LJ(A), p. 338; see also LJ(B), vi. 21. (LJ(A) and LJ(B) refer to different sets of lecture sets included in citation above.)

27 – Hume *Essays*, I, pp. 294–5 ('Of Commerce').

28 – Smith LJ(B), 300–301.

29 – *Boswell in Extremes*, p. 113; the 'system of needs' is in G. W. F. Hegel *Philosophy of Right* (Oxford: Clarendon Press, 1965) pp. 126–128, paragraphs 189–195.

30 – Hume *Essasys*, I, pp. 454–5 ('Of the Original Contract').

31 – Hume *Treatise*, pp. 41–46; see also Alastair MacIntyre *After Virtue: A Study in Moral Theory* (London: Ducksworth, 1981), pp. 45–54; also David Miller *Philosophy and Ideology in Hume's Political Thought* (Oxford: Clarendon Press, 1981), ch. 2.

32 – Hume *Treatise*, pp. 536–552.

33 – Hume *Enquiries*, pp. 80–89.

34 – Hume *Enquiries*, pp. 169–l74; 188; 214–218; *Essays*, I, p. 456.

35 – Hume *Essays*, II, pp. 109–113.

36 – MacIntyre *After Virtue*, p. 46.

37 – J. G. A. Pocock *The Machiavellian Moment: Florentine Political Thought and the Atlantic Republican Tradition* (Princeton: Princeton University Press, 1975), chs. 5–6 on the civic humanist tradition; on the saint and the citizen in English revolutionary thought of the 1640s, see Michael Walzer *The Revolution of the Saints* (London: Weidenfeld and Nicolson, 1966); see also Quentin Skinner *The Foundations of Modern Political Thought*, 2 vols. (Cambridge: Cambridge University Press, 1978), vol. 2, chs. 7 and 8; on Boswell's romance of the Highland chieftain, see James Boswell *The Journal of a Tour of the Hebrides with Samuel Johnson, LlD* (Oxford: Oxford University Press, 1970).

38 – Denis Diderot 'Supplément au Voyage de Bougainville' in *Oeuvres philosophiques* (Paris: Garnier, 1964), pp. 447–516; Abbé Guillaume Raynal *Histoire philosophique et politique des deux Indes* (Paris: Maspero, 1981); J. J. Rousseau *The Social Contract and Discourses* (London: J. M. Dent, 1973), pp. 1–27 ('A Discourse on the Arts and Sciences').

39 – Hume *Treatise*, p. 365: 'In general, we may remark, that the minds of men are mirrors to one another, not only because they reflect each other's emotions, but also because those rays of passions, sentiments and opinions may be often reverberated, and may decay away by insensible degrees.' On the general idea that relative desiring is insatiable see René Girard *Deceit, Desire and the Novel: Self and Other in Literary Structure* (Baltimore: Johns Hopkins Press, 1965), ch. 1.

40 – Hume *Treatise*, p. 402.

41 – Rousseau *Social Contract and Discourses*, p. 86 ('A Discourse on the Origin of Inequality').

42 – Smith TMS, VII.ii.4.9.

43 – Hume *Essays*, I, p. 222; *Treatise*, pp. 413–418.

44 – David Hume *Dialogues Concerning Natural Religion and the Natural History of Religion* (Oxford: Clarendon Press, 1976), p. 237; on Hume's religious thought, see J. C. A. Gaskin *Hume's Philosophy of Religion* (London: Macmillan, 1978).

45 – Hume *Dialogues*, p. 237.

46 – On Providentialism in general see Jacob Viner *The Role of Providence in the Social Order* (Philadelphia: American Philosophical Society, 1972); the great Providential optimist of the eighteenth-century Anglican church was Joseph Butler. See his *The Analogy of Religion, Natural and Revealed* (London: Everyman, 1906). Both Adam Smith and Jonathan Swift professed to see the marks of Providential design in the blindness of sexual desire, in its incapacity to predict consequences or take them into account. See TMS, II.i.5.16; Jonathan Swift *Gulliver's Travels and Selected Writings in Prose and Verse* (London: Nonesuch, 1946), pp. 465–7: 'Although reason were intended by Providence to govern our passions, yet it seems that in two points of the greatest moment to the being and continuance of the world, God hath intended our passions to prevail over our reason. The first is, the propagation of the species, since no wise man ever married from the dictates of reason. The other is, the love of life, which from the dictates of reason, every man would despise and wish at an end, or that it never had a beginning.' (Thoughts on Religion, no. 15). See Hume *Treatise*, p. 485.

47 – Hume *Treatise*, pp. 477–483; *Enquiries*, pp. 183–192.

48 – Hume *History of Religion*, p. 32.

49 – Hume *History of Religion*, p. 25.

50 – Hume *Dialogues*, p. 241.

51 – Kolakowski *Religion*, p. 10.

52 – Brown *Cult of the Saints*, ch. 1. I am indebted to Robert Scribner, Clare College, Cambridge, for this and other references in the history of religion.

53 – *Boswell in Extremes*.

54 – Hume *Essays*, I, p. 228.

55 – *Boswell in Extremes*, p. xviii.

56 – Keith Michael Baker *Condorcet: From Natural Philosophy to Social Physics* (Chicago: University of Chicago Press, 1975). J. A. N. C. Condorcet *Sketch for a Historical Picture of the Progress of the Human Mind* (London: Weidenfeld and Nicolson, 1955).

57 – Karl Marx and Friedrich Engels *On Religion* (Moscow: Progress

Publishers, 1975), pp. 38–52 ('Contribution to the Critique of Hegel's Philosophy of Law'). There is an important discussion of the religious derivation of Marx's language in the heritage of Lutheranism in Abraham Rotstein 'The World Upside Down', *Canadian Journal of Political and Social Theory*, pp. 2, 2, 1978, pp. 5–29.

58 – This point is made by Leszek Kolakowski in his *Main Currents of Marxism* (Oxford: Oxford University Press, 1981), 3 vols., vol. 1, p. 413: 'Man is wholly defined in purely social terms; the physical limitations of his being are scarcely noticed. Marxism takes little or no account of the fact that people are born and die, that they are men or women, young or old, healthy or sick; that they are genetically unequal, and that all these circumstances affect social development irrespective of class division, and set bounds to human plans for perfecting the world.'

59 – I am thinking particularly of Fräulein Elizabeth von R. in Sigmund Freud and Joseph Breuer *Studies on Hysteria* (London: Penguin, 1974), pp. 202–259.

60 – Albert Camus *The Outsider* (London: Penguin, 1969). See also the essay on Camus by Conor Cruise O'Brien *Camus* (London: Fontana, 1970).

61 – Hume *Treatise*, pp. 299–311.

CHAPTER 4 · THE MARKET AND THE REPUBLIC

1 – On primitive culture as a lost Eden, see J. E. Chamberlin *The Harrowing of Eden: White Attitudes toward North American Indians* (Toronto: Fitzhenry and Whiteside, 1975); on trading contact as a needs creation process see Arthur J. Ray *Indians in the Fur Trade, 1660–1870* (Toronto: University of Toronto Press, 1974); and A. J. Ray and D. Freeman *Give us Good Measure: An Economic Analysis of Relations between the Indians and the Hudson's Bay Company before 1763* (Toronto: University of Toronto Press, 1978); see also Marshall Sahlins *Culture and Practical Reason* (Chicago: University of Chicago Press, 1976), ch. 3.

2 – John Locke *Two Treatises of Government*, II, 49.

3 – Adam Smith 'Letter to the Editors of the Edinbugh Review' in *Essays on Philosophical Subjects* (Oxford: Oxford University Press, 1980), pp. 242–256. This source will be cited hereafter as EPS.

4 – Rousseau had Melon in mind. See Rousseau, *Social Contract and Discourses*, p. 16 ('Arts and Sciences').

5 – *Social Contract and Discourses*, p. 76 ('Inequality').

6 – Marshall Sahlins *Stone-Age Economics* (London: Tavistock, 1974),

pp. 1-39.

7 – Adam Smith *An Inquiry into the Nature and Causes of the Wealth of Nations* (Oxford: Oxford University Press, 1976) I.ii.2. This source cited hereafter as WN.

8 – Contrast Rousseau's views of sociability and language: 'Be the origins of language and society what they may, it may be at least inferred from the little care which nature has taken to unite mankind by mutual wants, and to facilitate the use of speech, that she has contributed little to make them sociable, and has put little of her own into all they have done to create such bonds of union. It is in fact impossible to conceive why, in a state of nature, one man should stand more in need of the assistance of another, than a monkey or a wolf of the assistance of another of its kind: or, granting that he did, what motives could induce that other to assist him; or even then, by what means they could agree upon the conditions.' Rousseau 'Inequality', p. 63. See also *Essai sur l'origine des langues* (Paris: Bibliothèque du Graphe, 1981). A reprint of the 1817 Paris edition.

9 – WN, V.i.b.i: LJ(B) 10; LJ(A)iv.21.

10 – Rousseau 'Inequality', p. 83.

11 – TMS, III.3.30.

12 – TMS, IV.1.10.

13 – WN, (1).4.

14 – Rousseau 'Inequality', p. 105.

15 – WN, I.i.11. This interpretation of these passages was developed in a joint paper with Istvan Hont 'Needs and Justice in the Wealth of Nations' in our *Wealth and Virtue: The Shaping of Political Economy in the Scottish Enlightenment* (Cambridge: Cambridge University Press, 1983), ch. 1. I am indebted to my colleague, Istvan Hont, for my understanding of Smith's work and its context.

16 – See his reply of 1753 to the King of Poland's strictures against the *Discourse on the Arts and Sciences*: 'The words rich and poor are relative: wherever men are equal, there are neither rich nor poor.' Quoted in Robert Wokler's essay in S. Harvey et al. *Re-Appraisals of Rousseau: Studies in Honour of R. A. Leigh* (Manchester: Manchester University Press, 1980), p. 268. See also 'Social Contract' in *Social Contract and Discourses*, p. 231 (III, ix).

17 – Rousseau 'Political Economy' in *Social Contract and Discourses*, p. 139.

18 – Quoted in Lester G. Crocker *Jean-Jacques Rousseau*, 2, vols. (New York: Macmillan, 1974), vol. 1, p. 271.

19 – 'Emile' in *Social Contract and Discourses*, p. 302.

20 – 'Political Economy', p. 146.

21 – 'Social Contract', p. 204 (II, xi).

22 – 'Social Contract', p. 217 (III, iv).

23 – For Rousseau's opposition to machinery see 'Fragments Politiques' in *Oeuvres Complètes*, 3 vols. (Paris: Gallimard, 1961), vol. 3, p. 525; on the town–country division of labour, see 'Political Economy', p. 149. Physiocratic economics, of course, was centrally concerned with balancing agricultural and manufacturing production. See R. L. Meek *The Economics of Physiocracy* (London: Allen and Unwin, 1964); Elizabeth Fox-Genovese *The Origins of Physiocracy: Economic Revolution and Social Order in 18th century France* (Ithaca, NY: Cornell University Press, 1976). For Smith's analysis of the town–country division of labour, see WN, III. i. i.

24 – Rousseau 'Social Contract', p. 205 (II, xi).

25 – The phrase 'only if everything changes, can everything stay the same' is taken, of course from T. de Lampedusa *The Leopard*, (Milan: Feltrinelli, 1963).

26 – I am indebted to John Pocock for the sense of the interconnection in eighteenth-century thought between the themes of civic personality, the growth of the state and the elaboration of a social division of labour. See his *Machiavellian Moment*, ch. 5.

27 – Rousseau 'Social Contract', p. 231 (III, ix).

28 – WN, I.iii.1–8.

29 – WN, IV.ix.49.

30 – WN, IV.ix.51.

31 – The best study of Smith's politics and the role of republican and civic humanist themes in his thought is Donald Winch *Adam Smith's Politics: An Essay in Historiographic Revision* (Cambridge: Cambridge University Press, 1978). Another excellent study of Smith's politics, emphasizing its roots in English political ideology, rather than in Renaissance civic humanism, is Duncan Forbes 'Scientific Whiggism: Adam Smith and John Millar', *Cambridge Journal*, VII (1954), pp. 643 –670; also 'Sceptical Whiggism, Commerce and Liberty' in A. S. Skinner and T. Wilson (eds.) *Essays on Adam Smith* (Oxford: University Press, 1976).

32 – WN, V.i.a.15.

33 – WN, V.i.f.51.

34 – WN, V.i.f.50.

35 – Rousseau 'Inequality', p. 104. On the theme of authenticity

in Rousseau see Marshall Berman *The Politics of Authenticity: Radical Individualism and the Emergence of Modern Society* (New York: Athenaeum, 1970); see also the best overall study of Rousseau's political and moral theory and its relation to his personality, J. N. Shklar *Men and Citizens: A Study of Rousseau's Social Theory* (Cambridge: Cambridge University Press, 1969).

36 – Rousseau 'Inequality', p. 86. See also Smith EPS, p. 252.

37 – Smith LJ(A), p. 333.

38 – LJ(A), p. 263.

39 – See especially Springborg *The Problem of Human Needs and the Critique of Civilization*, pp. 36–43; see also J. Starobinski *Jean-Jacques Rousseau: la transparence et l'obstacle* (Paris: Plon, 1958).

40 – Rousseau 'Inequality', p. 54.

41 – Rousseau 'Social Contract' p. 177 (I. viii).

42 – This point is made in Springborg *The Problem of Human Needs and the Critique of Civilization*, p. 119.

43 – WN, V.ii.k; WN, II.iii.28: '. . . the desire of bettering our condition, a desire which, though generally calm and dispassionate, comes with us from the womb, and never leaves us till we go into the grave. In the whole interval which separates those two moments, there is scarce perhaps a single instant in which any man is so perfectly and completely satisfied with his situation as to be without any wish of alteration or improvement of any kind.'

44 – WN, I, viii. 23–27: Thomas Malthus *An Essay on the Principle of Population* (London: Penguin, 1970), ch. XVI for Malthus's critique of Smith.

45 – WN, II, iii.36.

46 – J. H. Hexter 'Republic, Virtue, Liberty and the Political Universe of J. G. A. Pocock' in *On Historians* (London: Collins, 1979), pp. 255–303; see also J. G. A. Pocock 'Authority and Property: The Question of Liberal Origins' in B. C. Malamont (ed.) *After the Reformation: Essays in Honour of J. H. Hexter* (Manchester: Manchester University Press, 1980), pp. 331–354.

47 – On the relation between Rousseau and Marx, see Robert Wokler 'Rousseau and Marx' in David Miller and Larry Siedentop (eds.) *The Nature of Political Theory* (Oxford: Clarendon Press, 1983), pp. 219–246; see also G. della Volpe *Rousseau and Marx* (London: Lawrence and Wishart, 1978); Lucio Colletti *From Rousseau to Lenin* (London: New Left Books, 1972).

48 – Karl Marx 'Economic and Philosophical Manuscripts of 1844' in

Karl Marx and Friedrich Engels *Collected Works* (London: Lawrence and Wishart, 1975), vol. 3. I am indebted to the commentary on these passages in Agnes Heller *The Theory of Need in Marx*, passim.

49 – Karl Marx *Grundrisse: Foundations of the Critique of Political Economy* (London: Penguin, 1974), p. 401.

50 – Marx *Grundrisse*, pp. 401–409. I wish to acknowledge Kate Soper's commentary on these passages in *On Human Needs*, ch. 5; and C. Castoriadis *Crossroads in the Labyrinth* (Brighton: Harvester Press, 1983), pp. 260–340.

51 – A new approach to the politics of development is trying to find ways to increase the capacity of poor countries to satisfy their own basic needs, instead of launching into development strategies which subordinate the local economy to the international market. For an excellent guide to this literature see Richard Sandbrook *The Politics of Basic Needs: Urban Aspects of Assaulting Poverty in Africa* (London: Heinemann, 1982).

52 – See the essay by Istvan Hont 'The "rich country–poor country" debate in Scottish classical political economy' in our *Wealth and Virtue*, pp. 271–317.

53 – Giambattista Vico *Selected Writings* (Cambridge; Cambridge University Press, 1982).

CONCLUSION · HOMELESSNESS AND BELONGING

1 – See Fred Hirsch *Social Limits to Growth* (London: Routledge and Kegan Paul, 1977); also Lester C. Thurow *The Zero-Sum Society: Distribution and the Possibilities for Economic Change* (New York: Basic Books, 1980).

2 – See Eugen Weber *Peasants into Frenchmen: The Modernization of France, 1870–1914* (London Chatto and Windus, 1979); Maurice Agulhon *The Republic in the Village* (Cambridge: Cambridge University Press, 1982); Benedict Anderson *Imagined Communities: Reflections on the Origin and Spread of Nationalism* (London: Verso, 1983).

3 – See Marshall Berman's rich and fascinating discussion of modernism as a language of city life in *All That is Solid Melts Into Air: The Experience of Modernity* (New York: Simon and Schuster, 1982; London: Verso, 1983).

INDEX